We ♥ Cooking!

We ♥ Cooking!

Totally Tasty Food for Kids

Lilly and Audrey Andrews,
the Twin Chefs

To Auntie Debbie, whose love for family, parties,
and fun still inspires us every day.
We miss you. . . .

foreword

In a world where most parents don't let their kids use scissors unattended, and most kids will choose chicken nuggets over chickpeas every time, Lilly and Audrey fill me with optimism for their generation.

I first met the twins in Sonoma when they were seven years old. At that time, their parents allowed them to use knives, though the sharpest one was a dull steak knife. But the twins didn't allow that to dampen their unbridled enthusiasm or sense of wonderment in the kitchen.

Two years later, they cooked their first meal for me (with a little assistance from their parents): beef bourguignon over creamy polenta with a blood orange salad. It was delicious. I can still remember the pint-sized gourmets in their crisp little chef's jackets, beaming with sunshine energy, finishing each other's sentences, climbing on stools to reach the cupboard, whisking up a storm, licking fingers, and squealing in delight as it all came together. And afterwards, when most kids would have patted themselves on the back and run off to play video games, they pressed me for feedback on the flavors and presentation, eager to change things up on the next go-around.

Every time I have seen the twins since then, they bubble over with excitement about a new ingredient, dish, or technique that they've learned. Now 12 years old, they exude a passion and enthusiasm for cooking that is as contagious to adults as it is to kids. That passion is encapsulated in the recipes in this book, which focus on healthy ingredients and fresh flavors. Every recipe is unintimidating and easy to follow—yet so tasty it is sure to inspire kids and parents to expand their culinary horizons and spend more quality family time in the kitchen.

The twins' pure love of cooking and infectious enthusiasm have already earned them the role of the Pied Pipers of kids' cooking. With *We [heart] Cooking!*, Lilly and Audrey will be luring their new friends away from the precipice of processed foods and leading them on a joyous parade to the playground of nutritious deliciousness.

—Bob Blumer,
Host of *Surreal Gourmet*, *Glutton for Punishment*,
and *World's Weirdest Restaurants*

contents

love at first bite

We've never known a time when we didn't love being in the kitchen. When we were 3, Mom and Dad started showing us how to peel carrots, mix batter, and even hull strawberries. When we were 4, the highlight of our year was baking a batch of pumpkin muffins. Since we were so young (and short), we were not allowed to put the muffins in or take them out of the oven—Mom did that for us. But the idea of mixing up ingredients, then baking the batter and having treats to eat that we had made ourselves was like a total miracle.

We were hooked.

We were also super curious about how to make other things besides pumpkin muffins. We didn't know how to read yet, so we watched cooking shows. The second we saw someone making a new dish with ingredients we didn't recognize, we wanted to make it—immediately.

Our mom didn't realize just how crazy we were for cooking, but then she started adding up the receipts after she took us to the grocery store and farmer's market to get whatever new and different thing we wanted to cook with next. She put the kibosh on the shopping and said we had to start figuring out how to cook with what we found in the kitchen. "Necessity is the mother of invention," as she likes to say. And so we became masters of reinventing leftovers!

The bottom line is, we are totally lucky to have such awesome and supportive parents. We're also lucky that we live in California. There are lots of local farms here, and there are also tons of food people—chefs and food makers who are super passionate and like to share what they know with us. And now we feel even luckier to have the chance to share with you all the knowledge we've picked up on our amazing food adventure. The recipes, tips, shortcuts, and food facts in the pages of this book will hopefully get you started on your own amazing food adventure. We heart cooking—and we hope you will, too!

—Lilly and Audrey Andrews

cooking our way

The kitchen is a place to let your imagination run free. In other words, there isn't one right way to cook. But there are some basics you can master so you're prepared for anything a recipe might throw your way. And here's a piece of really important advice (for life, not just for the kitchen!): If you need help of any kind, ask for it. The kitchen is a magical place but is full of lots of sharp knives and big pots of boiling water! So don't take any chances. Got questions or concerns? Give a holler.

getting started

There's a fancy French phrase that describes getting ready to cook: mise en place (pronounced meez ahn plahs). It's French for "put everything in its place." We think of it as, "Set yourself up for success!" If the tomato is supposed to be diced, dice it ahead of time. If the butter has to be room temperature, take it out of the fridge so it can warm up while you're prepping other things. The point? Cooking's more fun when you have what you need when you need it.

giving 'em a scrub

Clean is good! Rinse fresh fruit, vegetables, and herbs in fresh water for at least 20 seconds before using them.

greens We have a special system for washing greens because it's super important to clean off dirt and pesticides. Fill your sink with fresh water, add your fresh lettuce or other greens, and swish them around to remove the gritty stuff. Then drain the sink and run cold water over the leaves. Send them spinning in the salad spinner to get the water off or pat them dry with a clean kitchen towel.

grating and zesting

If a recipe calls for "zest," you need to take the outer peel off a citrus fruit. You might want to get your hands on a cool tool called a "microplane grater" for this. (You can also use it for grating fresh ginger.) Slide the whole fruit back and forth on the cutting surface, being extra careful not to touch the rough part of the grater

(because, um, you're not trying to grate your fingers). Grate and use the colored part of the citrus peel but not the white part—the white part is usually bitter.

measuring just enough

Measuring can be kind of tricky. If you take the time to do it right, you increase the chances that you're going to make something awesome.

dry ingredients Spoon the dry ingredient into a measuring cup or spoon, and run the back of a table knife across it to get off the extra.

wet ingredients Put a liquid measuring cup on a flat surface. Bend down so the lines on the cup are at the same level as your eye. Pour liquid in until it reaches the measuring line you want.

cracking an egg

Cracking an egg is all about degrees! Whack it too hard and you'll end up with a fistful of raw egg. Tap it too softly and you'll have to hit it more than once, which means you'll probably end up with shell in your bowl. (Trust us, most recipes don't taste better with eggshell.) Instead, hold the egg in the palm of the hand you write with, your fingertips gently curled around it. Moving your hand from the wrist (don't lift your arm), crack the egg once on the rim of your bowl. Holding both ends of the cracked egg with your fingertips, gently open the egg, dropping the contents into the bowl.

separating the yolk from the white

Crack an egg using our instructions above—except for the last part about dropping the contents into the bowl. This time, when you open the shell, keep the contents inside one of the halves. Then try one of two techniques:

- Hold the halves over a bowl and carefully pour the yolk from shell half to shell half, letting the white fall into the bowl below. Or ...

- Hold a slotted spoon over a bowl. Pour the egg onto the spoon. The white will slip through the slots, leaving the yolk behind on the spoon.

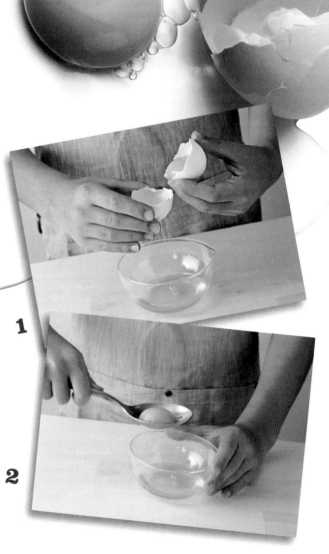

1

2

whisking

When you whisk, you stir quickly (but gently) using a tool made from wire or wooden reeds. Know what it's called? Yep, a whisk! Using the hand you write with, move the whisk back and forth quickly by bending your wrist. Keep your arm as still as you can.

we ♥ cooking!

knife techniques

Using knives is an important part of cooking, but it can be dangerous, so ask a grown-up to watch when you're cutting up ingredients. Here are some other tips that might help you.

- **Find the right knife for your hand.** How do you know if a knife is right for your hand? Good question. The handle should fit in your palm and not feel too heavy or hard to manage.

- **Use the right type of knife.** There are all sorts of knives for all sorts of foods. Cutting small things? Use a paring knife. Large things? A small chef's knife. If you're cutting tomatoes or something else with a soft skin, use a small, serrated knife.

- **Hold the knife the right way.** Hold the knife firmly in the hand you write with, gripping the handle with your fingers.

- **Hold the food the right way.** Hold the food you're cutting with your fingers curled, so your fingertips don't get in the way of the blade. (Practice this—it's super important!) Also, if you're cutting something round like an apple, cut it in half first. Then turn the halves over, cut side down. This will help you hold them as you cut.

chiffonade This is one of our faves because you can cut herbs and greens into ribbons, which look really cool! First, stack the leaves, then cut them crosswise into strips. For small leaves, stack first, then roll into a cylinder to steady them, then cut crosswise.

chopping Chopping is the old standby. When you chop, you cut food into uneven pieces. Using a small chef's knife, hold the handle with one hand and steady the blade point on the far side of the item you're cutting. Raise and lower the handle, moving the blade back and forth across the food while still holding the point in place.

dicing When you dice, you are making cubes, which should all be about the same size. First, cut the food into even slices, then stack them. Cut again to make strips, then cut the strips crosswise.

julienne Julienne strips are super skinny— they're the size of matchsticks. Let's say you're cutting a bell pepper into julienne strips. First remove the core and seeds (see page 16), then cut crosswise into halves. With the rounded side down, hold the pepper with curved fingers and cut thin slices that are about the same width.

mincing The technique for mincing is the same as chopping, but you just keep going until the pieces are super duper small!

we ♥ cooking! 15

cutting vegetables

Some vegetables have cores and seeds; others have leaves. This means you have to prepare them differently. Here's how.

seeding and coring bell & chile peppers

Use a paring knife to cut a slice from the bottom of the pepper. Place it cut side down to steady it. Hold the pepper by the stem, cutting from top to bottom, leaving the seeds at the center. Rotate the pepper and cut until you're left with the stem, core, and seeds, which you can get rid of.

seeding cucumbers

Using a paring knife, cut the cucumber lengthwise into halves. Grab a spoon, scrape out the seeds, then discard them.

slicing green onions

Trim the ends of your green onions with a chef's knife. Then stack as many as you can easily hold with one hand. Curve the fingers holding the onion (to protect them!) and cut the onion into slices.

slicing onions

Use a chef's knife to cut your onion in half through the stem end. Hold it cut side down, curve those fingers, and cut the onion crosswise into slices. The slices can be separated into half-rings.

trimming chard & kale

Pull the leaves off the bunch. Fold them in half along the center (called the "rib"). Cut the leafy parts away with a paring knife. Stack them and cut them crosswise into pieces.

watch the knife!

We figured out pretty fast that our hands are too small to hold a lot of the knives that grown-ups use. But so what? There are lots of different ways to slice and dice!

food processor The food processor is awesome! Just make sure you're using the right blade for the job and that an adult helps you install it. We like to use the chopping blade for mincing and pureeing onions and other vegetables. The slicing attachment is great for carrots and potatoes, and the julienne blade is amazing when we want to cut vegetables into matchstick-sized pieces. The food processor is a time saver, and it's also just cool to use!

kitchen shears Sometimes a pair of scissors is even better than a knife, like when you want to cut herbs, lettuce, or soft veggies into pieces.

mini chopper We love the mini chopper! It's our go-to tool for chopping and mincing all kinds of veggies and herbs. We cut the food into large chunks first, then put the chopper over the chunks. A few whacks on the plunge top, and our ingredient is chopped exactly the way we want.

pizza wheel Here's a secret: The pizza wheel is not just for pizza! You can chop vegetables by running it back and forth across them, or separate the leafy part of kale from the rib.

vegetable peeler Peelers are great for cutting super thin slices that are all the same size. Try this on veggies like zucchini.

using the stove

It took us a while to master these techniques. If you don't get them right away, don't worry. It's all about practicing. But do make sure an adult is around when you try these at home.

boil To make a liquid hot enough that bubbles rise to the surface and break.

sauté To cook food pretty fast in something hot like butter or oil, while stirring the whole time.

sear To cook an item fast so the surface gets brown and the juices are sealed in.

simmer To keep a liquid just below the point where it boils. Steam comes off it but only a few bubbles come to the surface.

stir-fry To cook food in a hot, oiled pan while stirring the whole time with a spatula. Most people use a pan called a wok for stir-frying, but you can use pretty much any frying pan.

and one more thing ...

There are a lot of things in this book besides our recipes because we want to share the cool tips, trade secrets, and short-cuts that we've learned from our parents, our friends, and our mentors. It's all part of this amazing and wild ride we've been on. Our mom, who has supported us every step of the way, has her own stories to tell, and you'll hear from both her and our dad in the "Mom's/Dad's Eye View" sections. We also included some of our favorite surprising food facts in our "4'real?" boxes, good ingredient factoids in our "Health Nut" segments, and flavor mash-ups in "Outrageous Tries!" Plus, we included a special chart in the back of the book that gives you the nutrition facts for every recipe.

As we're sure you've figured out by now, we love to share, so we wrote a whole chapter on par-tays! There are menus for an afternoon tea, a Halloween party with a salted chocolate fondue cauldron (what?!), an Italian block party, and a swanky Valentine's Day dinner. But whether you're looking for something for a party, a fancy dinner, or a movie-night sleepover, we'll keep our fingers crossed that you find stuff you can't wait to get into the kitchen to make. That would make us suuuuuper happy. Now go cook something!

fuel up

If you've ever wished you could just
eat breakfast food all day long, then
this chapter has your name on it.
Tropical smoothies, out-of-control red
velvet pancakes, crazy-good crêpes ...
you may never bother with lunch again!

creamy dreamy tropical smoothie

*Wish you were on the beach right now? One sip of our smoothie and you'll be there before you can say "Aloha." Coconut milk and Greek yogurt make this smoothie super creamy, and pineapple gives it a **sweeeeet** tropical kick.*

Hands-On Time: 5 min. Total Time: 5 min. Serves 4 (serving size: 1 cup)

4 teaspoons unsweetened shredded coconut for garnish (optional)

2 cups fresh or frozen pineapple chunks

1 cup plain low-fat Greek yogurt

1 cup light coconut milk

3 tablespoons honey

1 cup crushed ice or ice cubes

☐ **toast coconut (optional)** If you would like to garnish with coconut, toast it first. Heat a small skillet over medium heat and add coconut flakes. Cook, stirring frequently, for 1 to 2 minutes or until the flakes are golden brown.

☐ **blend smoothie** Place pineapple, yogurt, milk, honey, and ice in a blender. Process on high speed for about 60 seconds until smooth or desired consistency.

☐ **serve smoothie** Pour into tall glasses. Garnish each serving with 1 teaspoon of toasted shredded coconut, if desired. Serve immediately.

outrageous tries!

What else can you do with this creamy-dreamy wonder? Make ice pops! Pour the smoothie into ice-pop molds and freeze until solid. Want some "c-c-crunch" in your pop? Put toasted coconut in the mold before filling it.

berry berry warm quinoa cereal

*Our pal Chef Elizabeth Eckholt, from Sonoma, California, gave us a super cool recipe for hot cereal, and we like to make it with a grain called quinoa (pronounced KEEN-wah). Have you heard of it? If you haven't, this healthy, South American grain with the wild name cooks like oatmeal, tastes sort of nutty, and can be found **everywhere** these days!*

Hands-On Time: 10 min. Total Time: 25 min. Serves 6 (serving size: about ¾ cup)

1½ cups uncooked quinoa

2½ cups 1% low-fat milk or unsweetened almond milk

¼ teaspoon ground cinnamon

⅓ cup whole almonds

¼ cup unsweetened shredded coconut

2 tablespoons brown sugar

½ cup blueberries

½ cup raspberries

Maple syrup (optional)

❑**rinse quinoa** Place quinoa in a strainer, rinse with cold water, and let drain.

❑**cook quinoa** Place rinsed quinoa in a saucepan. Add milk and cinnamon. Bring to a boil over medium-high heat. Cover, reduce heat to low, and simmer for about 15 minutes or until most of the liquid is absorbed and a tiny string-like tail pops out from the round body of each little grain.

❑**add flavorings** While quinoa cooks, coarsely chop almonds. When quinoa is ready, add almonds, coconut, and brown sugar. Continue to cook an additional 3 to 5 minutes or until quinoa is tender.

❑**serve cereal** Spoon cereal into individual bowls and top with blueberries and raspberries. Drizzle with maple syrup, if desired.

Health Nut

People are *bonkers* for quinoa, and they have been for a while, going back to the ancient Inca Indians. Quinoa is the ultimate power food—¼ cup is as high in protein as 1 cup of milk, contains more fiber than just about any other grain, and is rich in iron, making it great for our bodies. Does it get any better than that?!

we ♥ cooking!   25

kale leaf frittatas to go

*Portable food is the greatest! These little guys are basically tiny to-go omelets. We eat them in the car when we're late for school ... which, of course, **never** happens!*

Hands-On Time: 22 min. Total Time: 42 min. Serves 6 (serving size: 2 frittatas)

Cooking spray

4 cups baby kale leaves, stems removed

4 (0.5-ounce) slices deli-smoked honey ham

4 green onions

6 large eggs

2 ounces Monterey Jack cheese, shredded (about ½ cup)

¼ cup 1% low-fat milk

½ teaspoon kosher salt

⅛ teaspoon ground white pepper

☐ **line muffin tins** Preheat oven to 375°. Coat a 12-cup muffin tin with cooking spray. Line each cup with an even layer of kale leaves. Roll each slice of deli ham into a cylinder. Cut rolls crosswise into ½-inch slices to make wheels. Arrange wheels over kale leaves, using about two wheels per muffin cup.

☐ **make filling** Trim roots and dark green tops from green onions. Chop white and light green parts. (You should have about ¼ cup chopped onions.) Combine eggs, cheese, milk, onion, kosher salt, and pepper in a medium bowl. Stir well with a whisk.

☐ **fill muffin cups** Using a ¼-cup measuring cup as a scoop, fill each muffin cup with about ¼ cup egg mixture.

☐ **bake frittatas** Bake for 15 minutes or until egg is set.

☐ **serve frittatas** Remove pan from oven. Let frittatas cool in pan for 5 minutes. Remove frittatas from pan and serve.

outrageous tries!

Want to change it up a bit? Go hunting in your fridge for alternative ingredients! Try chopped bacon instead of ham if you'd like your frittatas to have an extra crunch. Sauté red or orange bell peppers and throw them in for some eye-popping color. And if you're craving something just a little spicy, add some green chiles.

chilaquiles and eggs

Do you sometimes forget to chip-clip your bag of tortilla chips after snacking? Yes? Then you'll love our chilaquiles! Chilaquiles is a delicious Mexican dish that usually includes tortillas. We use stale tortilla chips instead—that way, you can say you left that bag open on purpose. A tip: If you're making breakfast, use eggs; if you're making dinner, use shredded chicken.

Hands-On Time: 27 min. Total Time: 27 min. Serves 6 (serving size: 1/6 of mixture)

2 large tomatoes

2 jalapeño peppers

1 cup organic vegetable broth

2 garlic cloves, peeled

1/4 teaspoon salt

1 tablespoon olive oil

1/4 cup red onion

4 cups tortilla chips (about 40 chips)

6 large eggs

1 ripe avocado, sliced

1/4 cup light sour cream

1 tablespoon finely chopped fresh cilantro

make sauce Coarsely chop tomatoes and place in a blender. Cut jalapeños lengthwise into halves, discard stems and seeds, and add to blender. Add broth, garlic, and salt to blender. Cover and process on high speed for 1 minute or until smooth. Set aside. Heat oil in a 12-inch sauté pan over medium-high heat. Add onion and cook, stirring occasionally, for 2 minutes or until just tender. Add tomato mixture to pan. Bring to a simmer. Reduce heat to medium-low and continue to simmer, uncovered, for 10 minutes, stirring occasionally.

add ingredients Add chips to pan and stir to coat with tomato mixture. Crack eggs one at a time over chips, evenly spacing them in a circle inside pan. Reduce heat to medium-low, cover, and cook for 5 to 7 minutes or until eggs are set but still runny in the centers. Remove pan from heat. Arrange slices of avocado over eggs. Top with dollops of sour cream and a sprinkle of cilantro. Serve immediately.

maple, bacon & egg crêpes

*We love surprising friends with awesome breakfasts after sleepovers. This rice-flour crêpe that we created especially for our bestie is, well, **outrageous!***

Hands-On Time: 30 min. Total Time: 55 min. Serves 6 (serving size: 1 crêpe)

maple bacon

4 slices bacon

1 tablespoon real maple syrup

⅛ teaspoon black pepper

crêpes

3 large eggs

¾ cup fat-free milk

1 tablespoon butter, melted

½ cup white rice flour

1½ tablespoons tapioca flour

2 tablespoons cornstarch

1 teaspoon sugar

⅛ teaspoon salt

Cooking spray

creamy egg filling

3 large eggs

2 tablespoons fresh parsley leaves

1 tablespoon chopped chives

½ cup fat-free milk

¼ teaspoon salt

❑ **cook bacon** Preheat oven to 350°. Place a wire rack on top of a sheet pan. Arrange bacon slices in single layer on rack. Brush maple syrup over bacon using a pastry brush, then sprinkle evenly with pepper. Bake bacon for 25 minutes or until crisp. Remove from oven and let cool, then chop coarsely, and set aside. Reduce oven temperature to 200°.

❑ **make crêpe batter and prepare egg filling mixture** To make crêpe batter, separate eggs, placing whites into a blender and yolks into a medium bowl. Set yolks aside for use in filling. Add milk and melted butter to egg whites in blender. In another bowl, combine white rice flour, tapioca flour, cornstarch, sugar, and salt. Pour flour mixture into blender. Process for about 30 seconds or until smooth. Let batter rest 15 minutes while you prepare egg filling mixture. To make egg filling, add eggs, parsley, chives, milk, and salt to reserved yolks in bowl. Whisk until blended. Set aside.

❑ **cook crêpes and cook egg filling** Lightly coat a 10-inch crêpe pan or skillet with cooking spray. Place pan over medium heat. Whisk crêpe batter until mixed. Add ¼ cup crêpe batter to pan and swirl to cover bottom. Cook until underside of crêpe is golden brown, 1 to 2 minutes. Using a thin, wide spatula, turn crêpe over, and cook 30 seconds or until set. Slip crêpe from pan onto a plate and keep warm in oven. Repeat until all batter has been used, whisking batter each time before adding it to pan. Return pan to medium heat. To cook filling, pour in egg mixture, and cook, gently stirring with a spatula, until eggs are cooked. Spoon egg filling evenly into the center of each crêpe; roll up. Arrange crêpes, seam sides down, on a serving plate. Sprinkle with chopped bacon.

how to make crêpes

1 First things first—put on a cool apron. Then brush the crêpe pan with melted butter.

2 Pour batter into the pan and swirl it around so it covers the bottom of the pan evenly.

3 Cook for a minute or two, then use a spatula to peek underneath. If the crêpe is golden brown, flip it over!

4 When the other side is golden brown, slide that deliciousness out of the pan and onto your plate. Fill the crêpes, then ... EAT!

we ❤ cooking!   31

banana almond butter french toast sandwich

Breakfast sandwiches get us excited about the day ahead—especially when our panini press is involved. But you don't need a press to make this tasty sandwich. Just cook it in a frying pan with some cooking spray and press on it with the back of a spatula. **Presto!** *(Get it?!)*

Hands-On Time: 20 min. Total Time: 20 min. Serves 4 (serving size: ½ sandwich)

2 large eggs

¼ cup unsweetened almond milk

2 teaspoons vanilla extract

¼ teaspoon ground cinnamon

2 tablespoons almond butter

4 teaspoons maple syrup

1 banana

4 (1.5-ounce) slices multi-grain bread

Cooking spray (optional)

❑ **mix batter** Crack eggs into a bowl. Add almond milk, vanilla, and cinnamon. Whisk to combine.

❑ **prepare sandwiches** Mix almond butter and maple syrup in a small bowl. Cut banana lengthwise into 4 thin slices, then cut slices crosswise into halves. Spread almond butter mixture evenly across bread slices. Top 2 bread slices with 4 slices of banana each. Place remaining 2 slices of bread over banana, sandwiching butter and bananas inside.

❑ **cook sandwiches** Heat a panini press to 425° or high heat. Dip sandwiches in egg mixture and let excess drip off. Lightly coat grill plates of panini press with cooking spray, if needed. Arrange sandwiches on press. Close panini press, pushing down gently to flatten. Cook 3 to 4 minutes or until sandwiches are browned on the outside and hot in the center.

❑ **serve sandwiches** Place sandwiches on a cutting board. Cut in half on a diagonal. Serve hot.

Elvis Presley, the famous hip-shaking King of Rock 'n' Roll, ate a peanut butter-and-banana sandwich nearly every day. But his sandwich was a little different from ours, and not just because of the peanut butter: He fried his in bacon fat! Yowza!

the twin chefs' y.o.l.o. board!

check out our dream board to see what we plan to do in the not-so-distant, like-maybe-tomorrow future...

"I want us to have our own cooking show!"
—Lilly

"I'm going to start a non-profit that inspires kids to read."
—Audrey

"I'm going to design a kids' clothing line."
—Audrey

yum!

"I dream of eating my way through Europe."
—Lilly

"I want to take a family road trip across the U.S. and Canada."

—Audrey

"Someday, I plan to write a novel."

—Lilly

too cool!

"I'm going to zip-line through a tropical rain forest!"

—Lilly

"My dream is to make the volleyball team."

—Audrey

omg!

red velvet pancakes

Red velvet pancakes sure kick things up a notch on a Saturday morning. Super sweet with cream cheese topping, these crimson beauties are perfect for Valentine's Day, your birthday, or just a regular day when you feel like rocking someone's world with bright red pancakes!

Hands-On Time: 25 min. Total Time: 25 min. Serves 4 (serving size: 2 pancakes, about 1 tablespoon cream cheese topping)

cream cheese topping

2 ounces $\frac{1}{3}$-less-fat cream cheese (about $\frac{1}{4}$ cup)

3 tablespoons fat-free Greek yogurt

3 teaspoons powdered sugar

pancake batter

1 cup all-purpose flour

$\frac{1}{4}$ cup sugar

2 tablespoons unsweetened cocoa powder

2 teaspoons baking powder

$\frac{1}{2}$ teaspoon salt

1 large egg

$\frac{3}{4}$ cup 1% low-fat milk

4 teaspoons red food coloring

❑**make topping** Place cream cheese in a small microwave-safe bowl. Microwave at HIGH for 15 to 20 seconds or until softened. Add yogurt and powdered sugar. Stir until mixed and slightly fluffy. Set aside.

❑**make pancake batter** Combine flour, sugar, cocoa powder, baking powder, and salt in a bowl and stir with a whisk. Crack egg into another bowl and beat lightly with a whisk. Whisk in milk, then gently stir in food coloring. Add flour mixture and stir with a spoon just until mixed.

❑**cook pancakes** Heat a nonstick griddle or frying pan over medium-high heat. Spoon about $\frac{1}{4}$ cup batter per pancake onto hot griddle or pan. Cook pancakes for 2 to 3 minutes or until tops are covered with bubbles and edges of pancakes begin to look dry. Using a spatula, flip pancakes over and continue to cook for an additional 2 to 3 minutes or until bottoms are lightly browned and centers are no longer runny. Repeat with remaining batter.

❑**serve** Serve pancakes with cream cheese topping.

puffy popovers with raw apple compote

Peek in the oven "porthole" and watch our pretty Puffy Popovers puff up and nearly pop! (Try saying that ten times fast.)

Hands-On Time: 10 min. Total Time: 40 min. Serves 6 (serving size: 2 popovers)

apple compote
1 medium-sized golden delicious apple

1 tablespoon honey

1 teaspoon orange rind

1 tablespoon fresh orange juice

1/2 teaspoon fresh lemon juice

popover batter
4 large eggs, at room temperature

1 1/2 cups 1% low-fat milk, at room temperature

2 teaspoons vanilla extract

1/2 teaspoon salt

1 cup all-purpose flour

Cooking spray

cream dollop
1/4 cup light sour cream

1 tablespoon brown sugar

1/8 teaspoon ground cinnamon

☐ **make compote** Cut apple into chunks and place in a food processor. Add honey, orange rind and juice, and lemon juice. Pulse until coarsely chopped. Place compote in a bowl and set aside.

☐ **prepare pan and make batter** Preheat oven to 400°. Place a 12-cup muffin tin in oven while oven preheats. Crack eggs into a blender. Process for about 10 seconds to blend. Add milk, vanilla, and salt and process for 10 more seconds. Add the flour and process for an additional 30 seconds or until smooth.

☐ **bake popovers and make dollop** Remove muffin tin from oven. Lightly coat muffin cups with cooking spray. Carefully pour enough batter into each muffin cup to fill ¾ full. Bake for 30 minutes or until popovers are puffed and edges are brown. While the popovers are baking, mix sour cream, brown sugar, and cinnamon in a small bowl. Set aside.

☐ **cool and serve** Carefully remove the popovers from the oven. Immediately turn out popovers onto a cooling rack. Using the tip of a knife, prick a tiny hole into the base of each popover to allow steam to escape. Gently split popovers open. Spoon about ¼ cup compote into each popover, then spoon a dollop of sour cream mixture on top. Serve.

Mom's EYE View

Hi, everyone! Just a thought: The food processor can be a lot for young chefs, so if it's new to your kids, supervise them closely.

jammin' oat muffins

Hi! It's me, Lilly. When I was six, I went to an amazing bakery called Muffin Street, and I fell in love ... with a Raspberry Cheesecake muffin! In honor of that life-changing muffin, meet the Jammin' Oat muffin, which has the same fab raspberry flavor, plus oats and maple syrup.

Hands-On Time: 10 min. Total Time: 46 min. Serves 12 (serving size: 1 muffin)

Cooking spray
1⅓ cups unbleached flour
¾ cup quick-cooking steel-cut oats
⅓ cup packed brown sugar
2 teaspoons baking powder
⅛ teaspoon salt
1 large egg
¾ cup 1% low-fat milk
¼ cup canola oil
¼ cup maple syrup
¼ cup raspberry preserves or jam

❑ **mix dry ingredients** Preheat oven to 400°. Lightly coat a 12-cup muffin tin with cooking spray and set aside. Combine flour, oats, brown sugar, baking powder, and salt in a bowl and stir to mix. Set aside.

❑ **mix wet ingredients** Crack egg into a bowl and beat lightly with fork. Add milk, canola oil, and maple syrup and mix well.

❑ **blend dry and wet ingredients** Pour egg mixture into flour mixture and stir until combined. (Mixture should still be lumpy and very wet.)

❑ **bake muffins** Spoon ⅓ cup batter into each muffin cup. Spoon 1 teaspoon preserves or jam into center of each cup of batter. Bake for about 16 minutes or until muffins spring back when touched lightly in centers. Let cool in pan for 5 minutes. Place muffins on a wire rack. Let cool 15 minutes before serving.

4 real?

You know the Muffin Man, from the song? He was *real!* He lived in Victorian England, and his job was to deliver fresh muffins to people's doors. His muffins were more like English muffins than what we have today, but if someone wrote a song about them, they must have been *delish!*

ranch-style potato hash

*There are more ways to make hash than there are stars in the sky. (Okay, we're exaggerating a **little**.) But no matter what ingredients you use, the key to making awesome hash is to dice everything to roughly the same size, and cook it all until brown.*

Hands-On Time: 12 min. Total Time: 40 min. Serves 6 (serving size: about ¾ cup)

1½ pounds Yukon gold potatoes

½ fennel bulb

1 small onion

½ orange or red bell pepper

1 tablespoon olive oil

1 teaspoon garlic powder

1 teaspoon paprika

½ teaspoon salt

1¼ cups organic vegetable broth

1 tablespoon fresh thyme

2 ounces cheddar cheese, shredded (about ½ cup)

☐**prepare vegetables** Cut potatoes into ½-inch dice. Set aside. Trim off root end and any feathery fronds from fennel bulb half. Cut fennel into ½-inch dice. Finely dice onion and bell pepper. Set aside.

☐**cook vegetables** Heat a large nonstick skillet over medium-high heat. Add oil and swirl to coat pan. Add potatoes and fennel. Cook for 4 minutes, stirring occasionally to brown evenly. Add onion, bell pepper, garlic powder, paprika, and salt. Cook for an additional 3 minutes, stirring occasionally. Add broth and thyme. Reduce heat to medium and simmer for about 25 minutes or until liquid has evaporated and potatoes are tender.

☐**add cheese** Sprinkle cheese over hash and turn off the heat. Let cheese melt for 3 to 5 minutes, then serve.

outrageous tries!

Don't let the fennel scare you! Even though it might look a little strange, with its rounded, greenish-white bulb, green stalks, and feathery fronds on top, there's nothing weird about it, we promise. It's used a lot in Italian cooking, and when paired with potatoes, fennel is out of this world!

snack-time madness

We get a little nutty about our snacks because, well, snacks are the most important meal of the day. Kidding! (Just wanted to make sure you were paying attention.) In this chapter you're going to learn how to make killer snacks with chai, goji berries, and tapenade, so hold on to your *toques.* (That's French for chef's hat.)

chai spiced milk steamer

Sure, we love hot chocolate—who doesn't? But we think this spiced, buzz-free milk steamer is even better. Sometimes, when it's cold outside, our mom sends us to school with thermoses of it. (She rocks!) The spices heat us up and send our chills packing.

Hands-On Time: 10 min. Total Time: 15 min. Serves 2 (serving size: 1 cup)

2 cups 2% reduced-fat milk
1 teaspoon vanilla extract
1 teaspoon ground cinnamon or 1 stick cinnamon, plus ground cinnamon for sprinkling
¼ teaspoon ground allspice or 2 allspice berries
¼ teaspoon ground cardamom or 2 cardamom pods
1 decaffeinated tea bag
1 tablespoon honey

❑ **heat milk** Heat milk in a small saucepan over medium heat, whisking frequently, until frothy and warm. (Do not boil.) Add vanilla.

❑ **add spices** If using ground spices, stir cinnamon, allspice, and cardamom into hot milk. If using whole spices, add cinnamon stick to milk. Crush allspice berries and cardamom pods with a mortar and pestle, contain crushed spices in a spice bag or tea ball, then add to milk.

❑ **add tea** Add tea bag to milk, lightly wrapping string around handle of pan. Turn off heat and let tea bag and spices steep for 5 minutes.

❑ **add honey** Remove tea bag (and whole spices, if using) from milk and discard. Whisk in honey.

❑ **serve** Pour steamed milk into 2 teacups. Garnish each serving with a dash of cinnamon and serve.

4'real?

People have been drinking chai, known for its natural healing properties, for a *loooong* time. Like, almost 5,000 years! In America, "chai" usually refers to Masala chai, which means "mixed spice tea." It's a blend of spices like peppercorn, cardamom, cinnamon, and ginger mixed with black tea, milk, and sweetener, and it is *beyond* delish.

munch mix

*Munch Mix is the ultimate snack, designed to give you **maximum** energy. (Say that out loud in a TV announcer's voice, just for fun.) The nuts are crunchy, the berries are sweet, and the graham crackers? A treat!*

Hands-On Time: 5 min. Total Time: 5 min. Serves 12 (serving size: $1/3$ cup)

1 cup roasted almonds, unsalted

1 cup dried coconut strips or flakes

1 cup all-natural chocolate chip bunny grahams

$1/2$ cup dried goji berries

$1/2$ cup dried blueberries

☐ **mix ingredients** Mix all ingredients in a bowl. To store for up to 1 week, place bunny grahams and remaining mix in separate air-tight containers; combine before serving.

Health Nut

Are you looking at this recipe and saying, "Um ... *what* is a goji berry?" If you are, you're probably not alone. Goji berries are packed with antioxidants, which are really good for you. They also boost energy and contain over 20 different vitamins and minerals, making them crazy nutritious. Take *that*, other foods—bam!

figgy chewy granola wheels

We slow-bake these awesome little wheels until they have a special toasted flavor that you won't find in granola snacks you buy at the store. Ours are jam-packed with figs, apricots, pecans, and other deliciousness, because that's just how we roll ...

Hands-On Time: 20 min. Total Time: 1 hr. 30 min. Serves 16 (serving size: 1 wheel)

$1/2$ cup maple syrup

$1/4$ cup water

$3/4$ cup organic raw golden flax seed

1 cup dried figs

$1/2$ cup dried apricots, rough chopped

$1/2$ cup almonds

$1/2$ cup pecans

1 cup old-fashioned rolled oats

1 cup shredded unsweetened coconut

1 teaspoon almond extract

2 teaspoons vanilla extract

1 teaspoon cinnamon

1 teaspoon salt

❑ **prepare baking sheet** Heat the oven to 300°. Line a 13 x 1 x 18–inch sheet pan with parchment paper and set aside.

❑ **prepare mixture** In a bowl, stir together maple syrup and $1/4$ cup water. Add the raw flax seed, stir, and set aside to soak for 30 minutes. In a food processor pulse-chop dried fruit into small pieces; put in a large bowl. Without washing the food processor, pulse-chop the nuts into small pieces; add to the bowl of dried fruit. Add the oats and coconut into the bowl; stir to combine. Use your hands to separate and break up large pieces of fruit and nuts.

❑ **spread mixture on the baking pan** In the bowl of flax seed that has been soaking, add almond extract, vanilla, cinnamon, and salt; stir. Pour the flax seed mixture into the bowl of nuts and fruit and stir until mixed evenly and the ingredients are moistened. Evenly spread the mixture onto the lined sheet pan and press to ¼-inch thickness, making sure that the mixture is tightly pressed down. We use the back of a metal spatula or large spoon.

❑ **bake mixture and cut into rounds** Bake for 45 minutes, until golden brown. Remove from the oven and let cool for 5 minutes. Carefully take a 2-inch round cutter and press down as close together as possible to form wheels. Let the wheels cool on the sheet pan. When cool, gently pull the wheels apart and store in an airtight container. We save all the yummy bits that are left on the pan in a mason jar to sprinkle onto yogurt and honey.

how to make granola wheels

1 Remember that water and maple syrup mixture you made? Soak the flax seeds in it for about 30 minutes while you prepare the remaining ingredients.

2 At the end of soaking time, you'll have ... glue! The flax seeds will have caused the mixture to thicken, creating "glue" that will hold the ingredients together.

3 Spread the mixture evenly onto a baking sheet lined with parchment paper, trying not to eat too much of it.

4 After baking, use 2-inch round cutters to make the "wheels." Remember to let them cool before you start popping 'em in your mouth!

apricot cheese poppers

Our older sister Kathryn goes nuts for this quick-to-fix snack—"I love Apricot Cheese Poppers so much, I'd like to swim in a pool of them!" (We'll get right on that, Kathryn.) Use fresh apricots in summer and dried ones in winter—your taste buds will flip either way.

Hands-On Time: 7 min. Total Time: 15 min. Serves 4 (serving size: 4 dried or 2 fresh poppers)

16 walnuts

16 dried apricot halves or 8 small fresh apricots

3 tablespoons crumbled blue cheese

1 tablespoon honey

☐ **toast walnuts (optional)** If you like walnuts lightly toasted, preheat oven to 350°. Place walnuts on a baking sheet. Bake for 8 minutes or until lightly toasted, stirring once.

☐ **halve apricots** If using fresh apricots, cut apricots in half. Remove and discard pits.

☐ **top apricots** Place apricots on a platter. If using fresh apricots, place cut sides up on platter. Spoon about ½ teaspoon blue cheese onto each apricot. Place 1 walnut on top of each cheese-filled apricot. Drizzle honey over poppers and serve.

outrageous tries!

There's a pattern to these scrumptious poppers. Just think fruit, cheese, nut, and drizzle, and then substitute in whatever ingredients your heart desires. For example, you could try half a fresh fig or a dried fig with a spoonful of goat cheese, a pecan, and honey, and grind a little black pepper on the top. Don't let our recipe hold you back—go nuts and get creative.

OMG!
we're at the Chef's Table

Have we mentioned how amazingly lucky we are, especially when it comes to getting to meet some of the world's greatest chefs? Here are a few bites of wisdom they generously shared with us. Eat it up!

"The first bite of every dish is taken with the eyes," says Sonoma chef and instructor Charles Holmes. We didn't get it right away, but we sure do now. The first thing you do to your food is look at it ... so it should look as good as it tastes!

"Make sure your plate is the same temperature as what you are serving," says Chef Bob Blumer of Food Network's *Surreal Gourmet*. "It keeps the food at the right temperature."

Food Network chef and cookbook author Michael Chiarello gave us a great pointer for cooking outside: "Make sure your campfire stick is plenty long!" You want to be a good distance from the fire.

We learned about wood-fired pizza from the one and only restaurant owner and celebrity chef Wolfgang Puck, who told us that you should *never overwork your pizza dough.*

Chef and culinary educator Elizabeth Eckholt took us on food field trips around northern California to see a cheesemaker, an oyster farm, and an olive press. "Cook with the best seasonal, fresh, local ingredients," she told us. This may seem obvious to grown-ups, but it wasn't to us when we first started cooking as little kids.

double-dip guacamole and tortilla chips

With your own personal wedge of scoopable avocado, you can double-dip in the guacamole all you want and not get in trouble! So how do you pull that off? If you grill an avocado, it gets soft enough to scoop right out of the skin with a chip. No mashing necessary, and it looks pretty cool, too.

Hands-On Time: 10 min. Total Time: 17 min. Serves 4 (serving size: ½ avocado each)

1 small tomato, chopped

½ small red onion, chopped

¼ cup cilantro leaves, chopped

½ jalapeño, seeded and minced (optional)

½ teaspoon salt, divided

Juice of 1 lime

1 teaspoon olive oil

¼ teaspoon chili powder

1 garlic clove, minced

2 ripe avocados, seeded and halved

4 corn tortillas cut into quarters

Canola cooking spray

☐ **make salsa** Combine tomatoes, red onions, cilantro, and jalapeño, if desired, in a small bowl, and stir. Add ¼ teaspoon salt and lime juice and set aside.

☐ **combine ingredients** In a small dish, stir together the olive oil, chili powder, and minced garlic, and, using a pastry brush, paint the flesh of the avocado with the seasoned oil. Set aside.

☐ **make tortilla chips** Heat the oven to 400° and place the tortilla pieces onto a baking sheet. Lightly spray the tortillas with cooking spray and then turn them over and spray the other side. Sprinkle the remaining ¼ teaspoon salt over the tortilla pieces. Bake for 7 to 8 minutes until turning golden; remove from the oven and set to cool.

☐ **cook avocados** Heat a grill pan or skillet to medium-high heat. Place the avocados flesh side down and cook for 1 minute, until nice grill marks appear. Using tongs, turn them over and cook for 1 additional minute. Place each avocado half in a small bowl and score it with a sharp knife into squares. Spoon the tomato salsa on top of each avocado half and serve with 4 tortilla chips each.

devilish eggs

We had kind of a funny realization recently: All this time we thought we were making deviled eggs, we were really making "angel" eggs! The recipe we were using didn't ask for hot sauce or mustard, so our eggs were missing that zesty kick. Well, we've made up for it here. This recipe uses mustard, herbs, and spices to turn our sweet "angel" eggs into delightfully delicious spicy "devils."

Hands-On Time: 30 min. Total Time: 30 min. Serves 8 (serving size: 2 egg halves)

8 large eggs

1/4 cup mayonnaise

3 tablespoons fat-free Greek yogurt

1 teaspoon Dijon mustard

1/2 teaspoon minced fresh tarragon, plus 16 small leaves for garnish

1/2 teaspoon minced fresh basil

1/4 teaspoon smoked paprika

1/4 teaspoon sea salt

1/4 teaspoon fresh lemon juice

1/4 teaspoon Tabasco sauce

1/8 teaspoon ground turmeric

1/8 teaspoon celery seed for garnish

☐ **hard boil eggs** Place eggs in a saucepan and cover with 1 inch of cold water. Bring to a boil over medium heat. Remove from heat, cover, and let stand for 12 minutes. Using a slotted spoon, transfer eggs to a bowl of cold water. Let cool for 2 minutes. Remove eggs from water. Crack eggs and remove shells.

☐ **make mayonnaise dressing** While eggs are cooking, mix together mayonnaise, yogurt, mustard, minced tarragon, basil, paprika, salt, lemon juice, Tabasco, and turmeric in a bowl. Cover and refrigerate.

☐ **mash yolks** Cut eggs lengthwise into halves. Remove yolks and transfer to a small bowl. Set whites aside. Mash yolks with a fork until smooth. Add mashed yolks to mayonnaise dressing and mix with the fork until blended.

☐ **fill whites** Spoon yolk mixture into a lock-top plastic bag. Snip off a corner from bag. Squeezing bag gently, pipe mayonnaise-yolk mixture into egg white shells. (Alternatively, use a spoon to scoop yolk mixture into shells.) Garnish each egg with a sprinkling of celery seed and a tarragon leaf.

pumpkin seed tapenade bruschetta

Bruschetta is toasted bread with a topping. Usually, the topping is made with tomatoes, but we use a secret weapon—pumpkin seeds! Our pumpkin-seed topping is light and crunchy, with a salty tang to it. It's great on these toasts, or on grilled fish or chicken, or on a spoon, in your mouth.

Hands-On Time: 10 min. Total Time: 23 min. Serves 6 (serving size: 2 bruschetta)

12 (¼-inch) slices diagonally cut French bread baguette

Olive oil cooking spray

1 cup roasted pumpkin seeds, salted

½ cup chopped bottled roasted red bell peppers

2 teaspoons extra-virgin olive oil

6 large basil leaves

1 small garlic clove

❏ **toast bread** Preheat oven to 350°. Arrange baguette slices in a single layer on a baking sheet. Lightly coat with cooking spray, turn slices over, and coat second sides. Bake for 11 to 13 minutes or until golden brown. Remove from the oven and let cool.

❏ **make tapenade** In a food processor, pulse pumpkin seeds until coarsely chopped. Add roasted red bell pepper, olive oil, basil, and garlic. Pulse for 20 seconds until mixture is combined.

❏ **top bruschetta** Spread pumpkin seed tapenade over each baguette slice. Arrange slices on a platter and serve.

Health Nut

We've always known that one of the best parts of Halloween is toasting pumpkin seeds for a post-pumpkin-carving snack. What we didn't know is that these seeds have healthy fats, antioxidants, and fiber and are loaded with stuff like magnesium, which is good for your heart, and zinc, which helps with immunity. Is there anything these little guys *don't* have?!

mini sesame asian tostadas

It's hard not to call these crispy wonton shells cute because, well, they are. They're also the perfect containers for our sweet and savory Asian salad. Make the shells and the salad in advance, then fill the shells right before serving.

Hands-On Time: 10 min. Total Time: 22 min. Serves 6 (serving size: 3 tostadas)

18 wonton wrappers

salad
Olive oil cooking spray
1 teaspoon sesame seeds
1 teaspoon black sesame seeds
1 small Napa cabbage
4 clementines
1 cup snow peas
2 green onions
¼ cup finely chopped fresh cilantro

dressing
1 (2-inch) piece fresh ginger
2 tablespoons dark sesame oil
¼ cup fresh lime juice
¼ cup honey
4 teaspoons Dijon mustard
4 teaspoons lower-sodium soy sauce
4 teaspoons seasoned rice vinegar

☐ **make tostada cups** Preheat oven to 350°. Lightly coat both sides of wrappers with cooking spray. Using bottom of a 12-cup muffin tin, place a wrapper over bottom of each muffin cup, making small upside-down bowls. (Cover 6 remaining wrappers with plastic wrap and set aside while first batch bakes.) Bake for 8 to 9 minutes or until golden, carefully patting down any bubbles with a fork half-way through baking. Cool wonton cups on wire rack. Repeat to mold and bake remaining wrappers.

☐ **toast sesame seeds** Place a small skillet over medium-low heat. Add sesame seeds, and toast, stirring often, for 3 to 5 minutes or until golden brown. Let cool.

☐ **prepare salad** Cut cabbage lengthwise into quarters, then cut crosswise into slices. Coarsely chop cabbage, then place in a large bowl. Peel clementines, separate into segments, and place segments in bowl with cabbage. Chop snow peas and add to bowl. Remove root ends of green onions and slice crosswise. Add onions to bowl along with cilantro. Toss gently to mix.

☐ **make dressing and dress salad** Using a vegetable peeler, remove peel from ginger. Grate enough ginger to make 4 teaspoons. Place grated ginger in a small container with a lid. Add sesame oil, lime juice, honey, mustard, soy sauce, and vinegar. Cover and shake to mix well. Pour dressing over salad and toss to coat evenly. Sprinkle sesame seeds over top and toss gently to mix.

☐ **fill tostada cups** Arrange cooled wonton cups on a platter. Fill shells with salad mixture, distributing it evenly. Serve immediately.

lunch faves

Don't just sit there and eat lunch—take a trip to Italy or Thailand while you're chowing down. We like cooking from all over the world, as you'll see here with our Caprese Open-Faced Sandwich and our Pad Thai Spring Rolls. Hop on the lunch jet and take off to somewhere exotic ... even if you can only stay until the bell rings!

grown-up
grilled cheese

There's no question—grilled cheese sandwiches are awesome, right? When they're gooey inside and crusty outside, nothing else compares. Well, we think ours takes things to the next level with a super gooey cheese called Gruyère (pronounced GRU-YAIR) and some sassy mango chutney. Warning: Your life may never be the same again.

Hands-On Time: 15 min. Total Time: 15 min. Serves 2 (serving size: ½ sandwich)

2 teaspoons butter, softened

2 (1-ounce) slices whole grain bread

2 ounces Gruyère cheese, coarsely grated

2 tablespoons mango chutney, apricot preserves, or fig jam

☐ **assemble sandwiches** Spread butter on one side of both slices of bread and place the bread on a cutting board with the buttered side down. Press the grated cheese onto one slice of the bread, spread chutney on the other, and press the two slices together.

☐ **cook sandwiches** Heat a skillet over medium-low heat. Add the sandwich to the pan. Cover the pan and cook for 3 to 4 minutes, checking occasionally to make sure it's not burning. Then remove the lid and press down on the sandwich with a spatula. When the bottom side is crusty golden brown, flip the sandwich with the spatula. Cook the other side, uncovered, until golden brown, for about 2 minutes longer. Remove from pan, cut sandwich in half, and serve.

caprese open-faced sandwich

The Italians make this dreamy salad called Caprese—it has mozzarella, tomatoes, and basil, and it's one of our faves. But when you put it on a warm crusty baguette, it becomes a total rock star! Eat it whole for lunch or cut it into smaller slices for snack-sized sandwiches.

Hands-On Time: 10 min. Total Time: 38 min. Serves 6 (serving size: 1 sandwich)

1 (8-ounce) sourdough baguette

3 large tomatoes

2 garlic cloves

1 tablespoon extra-virgin olive oil, plus 1 teaspoon

1/4 teaspoon salt

1/4 teaspoon ground pepper

12 slices pre-sliced fresh mozzarella

1 tablespoon balsamic vinegar

12 small basil leaves

❏**preheat oven** Preheat oven to 350°. Line a sheet pan with parchment paper and set aside.

❏**cut baguette** Cut baguette in half lengthwise. Keeping halves together, cut crosswise on the diagonal into thirds, making 6 pieces total.

❏**assemble sandwiches** Cut each tomato into 4 equal slices about 1/4-inch thick and set aside. Mince garlic cloves. Mix garlic and 1 tablespoon olive oil in a small bowl. Using a pastry brush, brush each piece of bread with garlic oil. Place 2 slices of tomato on each piece of bread, sprinkle with salt and pepper, then top with 2 slices mozzarella.

❏**bake sandwiches** Bake at 350° for 25 to 28 minutes or until cheese is melted and edges of bread are browned. Turn oven heat to broil and broil for 4 minutes or until cheese is bubbly and lightly browned.

❏**make vinaigrette** In a small bowl or cup, combine remaining 1 teaspoon olive oil and balsamic vinegar, stirring with a whisk.

❏**top sandwiches with vinaigrette and basil** Remove sandwiches from oven. Drizzle vinaigrette evenly over sandwiches. Let cool for 3 to 4 minutes. Sprinkle sandwiches with basil. Serve immediately.

cannellini bean and corn salad pita pocket

Have you ever wondered what to put in your pita pocket? That's easy—scoop some salad in there! Our Cannellini Bean and Corn Salad is pretty much perfect in a pita. And if you're on a roll with the improvising, swap red onion for white and sub out the cannellinis for garbanzos.

Hands-On Time: 12 min. Total Time: 1 hr. 12 min. Serves 6 (serving size: 1 pita half)

salad

1 (15.5-ounce) can cannellini beans

1 ear corn

1 Shishito or Anaheim chile pepper

1 cup cherry tomatoes

1/2 small onion

1/3 cup coarsely chopped fresh cilantro

1/2 teaspoon kosher salt

vinaigrette

1 garlic clove

2 tablespoons olive oil

2 teaspoons fresh lemon juice

1 teaspoon white wine vinegar

1/8 teaspoon ground black pepper

pita pockets

3 pita rounds, halved

6 romaine leaves

❏**prepare salad ingredients** Place beans in a colander, rinse with cold water, and let drain. Pour drained beans into a large salad bowl. Remove husk from corn, then pull away and discard silks. Stand corncob upright on a work surface. Cut along side of cob to remove kernels, rotating cob after each cut until all kernels are removed. (You should have about 3/4 cup kernels.) Add to salad bowl. Cut pepper in half and remove the stem, seeds, and ribs. Finely dice the pepper and add to salad bowl. Cut tomatoes into quarters and add to bowl. Finely chop onion. (You should have about 1/3 cup.) Add to bowl. Add cilantro and salt to bowl. Toss salad gently to mix. Set aside.

❏**mix vinaigrette** Finely mince garlic clove. Place minced garlic in a small jar with a tight-fitting lid. Add olive oil, lemon juice, vinegar, and black pepper. Shake until well mixed.

❏**toss salad and fill pita pockets** Pour vinaigrette over bean mixture and toss gently to coat. Cover and refrigerate for at least 1 hour. Place 1 romaine leaf in each pita half; spoon salad mixture evenly into each pocket.

twin chefs sushi rolls

Sushi looks so cool and complicated, doesn't it? But don't worry, these rolls are easy to make, and they taste like they came from your local sushi bar. You can use white or brown rice—chef's choice. Make them at night, store them in the fridge, and give yourself a gourmet lunch the next day.

Hands-On Time: 14 min. Total Time: 14 min. Serves 2 (serving size: 8 pieces)

½ cup brown rice

1 (1-inch) piece fresh ginger

2 tablespoons ⅓-less-fat cream cheese, softened

½ teaspoon wasabi powder (dried Japanese horseradish)

½ English cucumber

2 ounces smoked salmon

½ avocado

2 nori (seaweed sheets)

2 tablespoons lower-sodium soy sauce

❏ **cook rice** Cook rice according to package directions. Let cool.

❏ **make seasoning mixture** Using a vegetable peeler or small knife, remove peel from ginger. Grate enough ginger to make 4 teaspoons. Place grated ginger in a small bowl; add cream cheese and wasabi powder. Stir until blended. Spoon mixture into a small lock-top plastic bag. Set aside.

❏ **prepare filling ingredients** Cut cucumber in half lengthwise. Using a spoon, scrape out seeds and discard. Cut cucumber into julienne strips. Cut salmon into ½-inch-wide strips. Cut avocado into thin slices. Set all aside.

❏ **roll sushi** Follow the instructions for how to roll sushi (opposite). Let rest, seam side down, for 5 minutes. Meanwhile, repeat to form second sushi roll.

❏ **cut sushi** Using a sharp knife dampened in water, cut each sushi roll crosswise into 8 (1–inch) rounds. Make sure to moisten knife after each cut. Serve sushi immediately with a side of lower-sodium soy sauce for dipping.

how to roll sushi

1 Lay out a sushi mat on a clean work surface. Place 1 sheet of nori on mat. Using clean, damp hands, spread ½ cup cooked rice over nori, leaving a 1-inch border. (Don't skimp on this—you'll need this border!)

2 Pipe half of cream cheese mixture in a line across middle of rice. Stack half the cucumber, salmon, and avocado in rows over cheese, firmly. Lift edge of sushi mat closest to you.

3 Fold lifted edge of sushi mat over filling and roll toward top edge, pressing firmly. Continue rolling toward top edge. Press mat to seal roll. Let rest, seam side down, for 5 minutes.

4 Fill a shallow bowl of water. Dip knife in water. Cut sushi crosswise into 8 rounds, dipping the knife into the water after each cut. Congrats! You just rolled sushi!

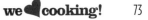

we ♥ cooking!

take it with you

If you're like us, you take food with you *everywhere*. The key is the right container. We've got some faves to tell you about.

In Japan, people use Bento Boxes for their home-packed meals. They're awesome for transporting lots of little snacks because the boxes have separate compartments. This way, when you're on the move, you don't have to worry about everything getting mixed up.

Canning jars come in different sizes, and—bonus!—they're dripless. We use the big guys for layering yogurt parfaits, the medium ones for sliced veggies like bell peppers and carrots, and the small ones for things like dressings and hummus.

Thermal containers are basically magic—they keep hot things hot and cold things cold! (Okay, it's physics, not magic, but still.) Pre-fill them with ice water to keep your salads and sushi cool, and hot water to keep your soups and pastas nice and toasty.

Tiffins are sort of like Bento Boxes in that they have separate compartments, but they're stacked, not side by side. We take Tiffins to school with snacks in one container and lunch in another. *Love* them!

we ❤ cooking!

pad thai spring rolls

We love the noodle dish Pad Thai so much, we invented an easy way to eat it at school. We took our favorite ingredients and rolled them in the rice paper wrappers used for spring rolls! A storage tip: If you wrap a roll in a damp paper towel and seal it in a plastic bag, it'll stay fresh for hours.

Hands-On Time: 22 min. Total Time: 22 min. Serves 6 (serving size: 2 roll halves)

peanut sauce

- 1/4 cup light coconut milk
- 3 tablespoons creamy peanut butter
- 1 tablespoon lower-sodium soy sauce
- 1 tablespoon fresh lime juice
- 1 tablespoon brown sugar
- 1/2 teaspoon red pepper flakes

rolls

- 4 ounces rice noodles
- 8 ounces shrimp, cooked and peeled
- 1/2 cup angel hair slaw
- 1 large carrot
- 1/2 cup fresh mint leaves
- 1/2 cup fresh cilantro leaves
- 1/3 cup roasted peanuts
- 6 (8-inch) round sheets rice paper

❑ **make peanut sauce** Combine coconut milk, peanut butter, soy sauce, lime juice, brown sugar, and red pepper flakes in a small bowl. Stir until blended. Set aside.

❑ **prepare filling** Cook rice noodles according to package directions. Drain and place in a bowl. Add 1/4 cup peanut sauce to noodles. (Cover remaining sauce and set aside for serving.) Toss noodles to coat evenly with sauce. Place bowl of noodles next to a clean work surface while you ready remaining ingredients. Place shrimp and slaw in small bowls. Peel and shred carrot. (You should have about 1/2 cup.) Place in a small bowl. Rinse mint and cilantro leaves and pat dry with paper towels. Place in small bowls. Coarsely chop peanuts and place in a small bowl. Place all bowls next to noodles and within easy access of clean work surface.

❑ **make rolls** Add hot water to a large, shallow dish to a depth of 1 inch. Follow the instructions for how to make spring rolls (opposite). Repeat to fill and roll all rice paper sheets. Gently cut each roll in half and serve immediately with reserved peanut sauce.

we ♥ cooking!

how to roll spring rolls

1 The rice paper sheets have to be soft before you can work with them, so soak them in hot water for 30 seconds. Then they'll be ready to rock 'n' roll!

2 Place a rice paper sheet on your work surface. Beginning at the end close to you, layer noodles, shrimp, slaw, carrots, mint, cilantro, and peanuts along the bottom third. Use about ⅙ of the contents from each bowl, leaving a ½-inch border uncovered.

3 Fold the bottom over the filling, pressing gently into a cylinder shape.

4 Fold in the sides, then roll from bottom to top. Place the rolls, seam side down, on a serving platter. Cover with a damp paper towel ... and admire your work!

we ♥ cooking!

rotisserie chicken salad lettuce cups

*Too busy to cook chicken for your chicken salad? No worries. Go to the store, get a rotisserie chicken, and add pomegranate seeds, toasted walnuts, and fresh flat-leaf parsley for some serious crunch. And forget about bread—this chicken salad goes in lettuce cups, which makes the flavors really **pop!***

Hands-On Time: 25 min. Total Time: 25 min. Serves 6 (serving size: 1 lettuce cup)

1 rotisserie chicken

1/4 cup chopped walnuts

1/4 cup light mayonnaise

1/4 cup fat-free Greek yogurt

2 teaspoons sherry vinegar

1/4 teaspoon kosher salt

1/4 teaspoon freshly ground black pepper

6 green onions

2 tablespoons finely chopped fresh flat-leaf parsley

1 head butter lettuce, rinsed and patted dry

1/3 cup fresh or dried pomegranate seeds

❑**shred chicken** Remove breast meat from chicken; discard skin. Shred chicken into bite-sized pieces. (You should have about 2 cups.) Place shredded chicken in a bowl, cover, and refrigerate until well chilled.

❑**toast walnuts** Preheat oven to 350°. Spread walnuts on a baking sheet. Bake for 5 minutes until lightly toasted. Let cool.

❑**prepare dressing** In a bowl, stir together mayonnaise, yogurt, vinegar, salt, and pepper. Set aside.

❑**make salad** Using a knife, chop white and light green parts of green onions. (You should have about 1/3 cup.) Add chopped onions to chilled chicken in bowl. Add walnuts to bowl. Mix in parsley. Add dressing and stir until evenly combined.

❑**fill lettuce cups** Put 1 lettuce leaf in each of 6 bowls. Top each lettuce leaf with a spoonful of chicken salad, sprinkle with pomegranate seeds, and serve.

thanksgiving wrap

Our Thanksgiving Wrap reminds us how much we have to be thankful for, even if we're eating it in the summer. It combines the holiday flavors we love—turkey and cranberries—with lettuce for some extra crunch.

Hands-On Time: 4 min. Total Time: 4 min. Serves 4 (serving size: ½ wrap)

4 romaine lettuce
leaves

2 (10-inch) spinach
tortillas

6 tablespoons garlic-
and-herb spreadable
cheese

4 tablespoons dried
cranberries

4 (1-ounce) slices roast
turkey breast

❏**chop lettuce** Rinse romaine leaves and pat dry with paper towels. Coarsely chop romaine. Set aside.

❏**fill tortilla** Lay tortillas in a single layer on a clean work surface. Spread cheese over one side of each tortilla, dividing it evenly and leaving a ½-inch edge. Sprinkle cranberries over cheese, dividing them evenly. Arrange 2 turkey slices in a single layer over each tortilla, then top each with ½ of the chopped lettuce in a single layer.

❏**fold tortilla** Working with 1 wrap at a time, fold in sides 1 inch. Fold up bottom and continue rolling away from you to enclose filling. Spread a tiny bit of cheese mixture on inside of top edge if necessary to keep wrap closed. Repeat to roll up remaining wrap.

❏**serve wraps** Cut wraps in half and serve.

outrageous tries!

Not in the mood for Thanksgiving? This wrap transforms like a pro. Let's say you love Indian food. Instead of a spinach tortilla, use whole wheat, and replace the turkey with roasted chicken. Lose the spreadable cheese and sprinkle curry powder in mayonnaise instead. Add golden raisins and grated carrots, and you're rocking a whole other wrap!

radiatore minestrone soup

*Once, our **entire** family was home sick, so we decided to make soup. We grabbed veggies from the fridge and **radiatore** pasta, which looks like a car radiator and has perfect broth-catching nooks and crannies. **Sluuurp** ....*

Hands-On Time: 30 min. Total Time: 50 min. Serves 6 (serving size: about 1½ cups)

2 carrots

1 small onion

1 small leek, white part only

5 Brussels sprouts

1 garlic clove

2 tablespoons olive oil

1 (16-ounce) can white beans, rinsed

6 cups organic vegetable broth

1 (14.5-ounce) can diced tomatoes

2 bay leaves

2 teaspoons dried oregano

¼ teaspoon ground white pepper

¼ teaspoon salt

¼ teaspoon red pepper flakes (optional)

2 cups (about 5 ounces) uncooked radiatore pasta

1 tablespoon chopped fresh flat-leaf parsley (optional)

❑ **prepare vegetables** Using a sharp knife or food processor, thinly slice carrots and set aside. (You should have about 1 cup.) Chop the onion (about 1 cup chopped) and leek (about ½ cup chopped). Cut each Brussels sprout in half lengthwise, then cut crosswise into very thin slices to make chiffonade. (See technique, page 15.) Mince the garlic.

❑ **cook vegetables** Heat olive oil in a large soup pot over medium-high heat. Add onion and carrot and sauté, stirring often, for 3 minutes. Add leek, Brussels sprouts, and garlic. Cook, stirring occasionally, for an additional 2 minutes. Meanwhile, place beans in a colander and rinse with running water.

❑ **make soup and serve** Add vegetable broth and undrained tomatoes to the vegetables. Stir in bay leaves, oregano, white pepper, salt, and red pepper flakes, if desired. Cook for 5 minutes. Add pasta and rinsed beans. Bring to a boil over high heat. Reduce heat to medium-low and simmer for about 15 minutes or until pasta is al dente (just tender to the bite). Carefully remove bay leaves. Ladle soup into bowls. Sprinkle with parsley, if desired.

Mom's EYE View

The rule in our house is to use up as much food in the kitchen as possible before going shopping for more. Over the years, the girls have honed their leftovers technique by creating soups and stews, and their adventurous combinations usually taste really good. (They're also a huge help at mealtime!) I highly recommend cooking with leftovers—it's a great, low-stakes way to get comfortable in the kitchen.

easy-peasy soup
with lemon zest

*We're not kidding about this soup being "easy-peasy"—we can whip up a batch before we go to school in the morning and eat it for lunch that day. When we crack open our thermoses, we feel like we're dining at a fancy bistro that just happens to be in the middle of our lunchroom! If you like herbs, go **super** fancy and throw in a tablespoon of tarragon, basil, or thyme when you're blending.*

Hands-On Time: 5 min. Total Time: 5 min. Serves 2 (serving size: about 1 cup)

1 (9-ounce) bag frozen sweet peas

$1/2$ teaspoon grated lemon zest, plus more for garnish

$1/8$ teaspoon salt

1 cup vegetable broth

2 tablespoons organic light sour cream

☐ **blend soup** Place peas, $1/2$ teaspoon lemon zest, and salt in a blender. Set aside. Pour broth into a microwave-safe cup or bowl. Microwave at HIGH for 60 seconds or until warm. Add warm broth to blender. Process on high speed for at least 1 minute or until soup is smooth.

☐ **serve soup** If serving soup cold, divide soup into 2 bowls and refrigerate until well chilled. If serving soup hot, divide into 2 large microwave-safe mugs or bowls and microwave at HIGH for 30 to 60 seconds or until hot. Top each cold or hot serving with 1 tablespoon sour cream and sprinkle with lemon zest.

Mom's EYE View

Usually, you cook a soup's ingredients, let them cool, and then puree before serving it. But the girls used to be so excited about their latest kitchen creation that waiting for anything to cool was pretty painful for them! Now, they've come up with a way to make the process a whole lot easier and safer—they combine cold pea puree with hot broth for a soup that's just right.

what's sup?

Usually, we start thinking about what we want to make for dinner right after we finish lunch. (Yeah, we're a little food obsessed, but in a *good* way!) Here, we offer up fish-on-a-stick and mini meatloaves made in a muffin tin. Crazy? Maybe. Awesomely delicious? For sure!

chicken curry bar

*The great thing about a curry bar is that there's something for everyone,
so even picky eaters are happy!*

Hands-On Time: 19 min. Total Time: 34 min. Serves 8 (serving size: ½ cup rice, about ¾ cup
curry mixture)

1⅓ cups uncooked dry brown rice

½ cup coconut strips or flakes

½ cup slivered almonds

3 green onions

½ cup golden raisins

½ cup dried banana chips

¼ cup chopped fresh cilantro leaves

8 lime wedges

2 pounds skinless, boneless chicken thighs

1 large onion

2 garlic cloves

1 tablespoon coconut oil

2 teaspoons curry powder

1 teaspoon salt

1 cup fat-free, lower-sodium chicken broth

1 cup light coconut milk

½ teaspoon red pepper flakes

¼ cup mint leaves

☐ **cook rice** Cook rice according to package directions. Remove from heat. Cover to keep warm.

☐ **prepare toppings** Heat a small skillet over medium heat. Add coconut and toast for 1 to 2 minutes or until mostly golden brown, stirring frequently. Place in a small serving bowl. Set aside. Return skillet to medium heat. Add almonds and toast for about 3 minutes or until golden, stirring frequently. Place in another small serving bowl. Set aside. Trim green onions, then stack and cut crosswise into thin slices. (You should have about ½ cup sliced onion.) Place in another small serving bowl. Set aside. Place remaining toppings (except for mint) in separate small serving bowls: raisins, banana chips, cilantro, and lime wedges. Set all aside until ready to serve.

☐ **prepare curry ingredients** Cut chicken into 1-inch-thick slices. Set aside. Cut onion in half through stem end. Place halves, cut sides down, on cutting board. Beginning at stem end, cut onion into thin slices. Mince garlic.

☐ **cook curry** Heat coconut oil in a large sauté pan over medium-high heat. Add onion and garlic, and sauté for 5 minutes or until beginning to caramelize, stirring often. Add chicken, curry powder, and salt. Stir to evenly coat chicken with curry powder. Cook for 7 minutes or until chicken is cooked throughout, stirring occasionally. Add chicken broth, coconut milk, and red pepper flakes and bring to a boil. Reduce heat to medium-low and simmer for 15 minutes or until sauce has thickened slightly, stirring occasionally.

☐ **serve curry** Just before serving, stack mint leaves, roll up tightly, and thinly slice crosswise into chiffonade. (See technique, page 15.) Place mint into a small serving bowl. Arrange serving bowls with toppings. To serve, spoon ½ cup rice into each of 8 individual shallow bowls and top each serving with about ¾ cup chicken curry. Serve immediately, allowing guests to add toppings of their choice.

mini turkey meatloaves

When we decided meatloaf needed a makeover, we went straight for our muffin tins. Yup, you heard us—mini turkey meatloaves in muffin tins! This underestimated weeknight dish is now totally ready for Instagram. —Lilly

Hands-On Time: 10 min. Total Time: 58 min. Serves 6 (serving size: 2 mini meatloaves)

½ small onion

2 pounds ground turkey

½ cup old-fashioned rolled oats

½ cup grated Parmesan cheese

2 large eggs

2 tablespoons 1% low-fat milk

2 tablespoons chopped fresh parsley

2 garlic cloves, minced

½ teaspoon red pepper flakes

½ teaspoon ground black pepper

½ teaspoon salt

Cooking spray

¾ cup ketchup

¼ cup barbecue sauce

6 slices center-cut bacon

❑ **mix turkey and flavorings** Preheat oven to 350°. Finely chop onion. (You should have about ½ cup.) Combine onion with ground turkey, oats, and Parmesan cheese in a large bowl. Mix well with your hands to distribute ingredients evenly. In a small bowl, combine eggs, milk, parsley, garlic, red pepper flakes, pepper, and salt, stirring with a whisk. Pour egg mixture over turkey mixture and mix with your hands until combined.

❑ **choose your pan size** To bake in muffin cups, lightly coat each cup of a 12-cup muffin tin with cooking spray. Place an equal amount of turkey mixture into each cup, filling each ¾ full. To bake in a loaf pan, lightly coat a 4 x 8–inch loaf pan with cooking spray. Place turkey mixture in pan and smooth top.

❑ **top with sauce and bacon** Mix ketchup and barbecue sauce in a small bowl. Spoon evenly over turkey mixture, dividing it equally if using muffin cups. Top with bacon, cutting each strip in half crosswise or laying strips in a lengthwise layer over a large loaf or to distribute equally over muffin cups.

❑ **bake** Bake until a meat thermometer inserted into center(s) reaches 165°, about 35 minutes for muffin-sized loaves and 55 minutes for a large loaf. Turn oven to broil. Broil 6 inches from heat for 3 to 5 minutes or until bacon is crisp and browned. Remove from oven and let sit 10 minutes before serving.

chicken and sausage paella

*There's a traditional dish in Spain called **paella** (pronounced pie-AY-uh) made with rice, meat, and vegetables, and it's usually flavored with a spice called saffron, which comes from crocus flowers—super cool, right? There are a lot of ingredients for this dish, so we cut, measure, and organize everything before we start to cook.*

Hands-On Time: 30 min. Total Time: 40 min. Serves 8 (serving size: 1/8 of mixture)

1 yellow bell pepper

1 red bell pepper

1 small onion

2 carrots

4 skinless, boneless chicken thighs

12 ounces turkey kielbasa

2 tablespoons olive oil, divided

2 teaspoons smoked paprika

1 teaspoon kosher salt

1 teaspoon ground black pepper

1 1/4 cups Arborio rice

3 garlic cloves

1 teaspoon saffron

1 teaspoon thyme leaves

1 bay leaf

3 1/2 cups fat-free, lower-sodium chicken broth

1/2 cup frozen or fresh sweet peas, thawed if frozen

1/2 cup chopped fresh parsley

☐ **prepare ingredients** Using a food processor, mini chopper, or sharp knife, mince yellow pepper, red pepper, onion, and carrots. Set aside. Using a knife, cut chicken thighs into 1-inch cubes and kielbasa into 1/2-inch slices.

☐ **cook meat and vegetables** Heat a large stainless-steel skillet over high heat. Add 1 tablespoon oil to pan and swirl to coat. Add chicken and sauté for 5 minutes or until browned. Add sausage and paprika and sauté for 4 minutes or until sausage is browned. Using a slotted spoon, transfer chicken and sausage to a bowl and set aside. Add remaining 1 tablespoon olive oil to pan. Add bell peppers, onion, carrot, salt, and pepper. Sauté for 1 minute. Add Arborio rice, garlic, saffron, thyme, and bay leaf. Continue to sauté for an additional 1 minute.

☐ **cook rice** Add chicken broth and bring to a simmer over high heat. Reduce heat to medium and continue to simmer for an additional 10 minutes or until rice is tender, stirring frequently.

☐ **combine all ingredients** Stir in peas, chicken, and sausage. Cook for an additional 3 minutes until thoroughly heated. Remove bay leaf.

☐ **serve** Sprinkle with parsley. Serve in shallow bowls.

sole in parchment pouches

*Cooking in parchment seals in juicy flavors **and** makes your food look like a present! Just gather your ingredients, wrap, cook, unwrap (yay!), and eat.*

Hands-On Time: 15 min. Total Time: 35 min. Serves 4 (serving size: 1 pouch)

1 bunch Swiss chard

4 (6-ounce) sole fillets

2 tablespoons olive oil, divided

$1/2$ teaspoon salt, divided

$1/8$ teaspoon freshly ground black pepper

1 lemon

4 thyme sprigs

2 tablespoons pine nuts

4 teaspoons white wine or organic vegetable broth

❏**prepare chard** Remove chard leaves from head. Cut away any tough stems and discard. Coarsely chop leaves. Rinse and spin dry in salad spinner or pat dry with paper towels. (You should have 7–8 cups chopped chard.) Set aside.

❏**prepare parchment** Cut 4 (12-inch) squares parchment paper. Set aside. Position oven rack in center of oven. Preheat oven to 450°.

❏**oil fish and chard** Place fish fillets in a bowl. Drizzle 1 tablespoon olive oil over fillets and toss gently with your hands until evenly coated. Set aside. Place chard in a large bowl. Drizzle with remaining 1 tablespoon olive oil and toss to coat. Sprinkle with $1/4$ teaspoon salt and $1/8$ teaspoon pepper, toss again, and set aside.

❏**wrap in parchment** Cut lemon into thin slices. Set aside. Lay parchment in a single layer on a clean work surface. Place equal amounts of chard in center of each square. Top each mound of chard with equal amount of fish. Sprinkle remaining $1/4$ teaspoon salt evenly over fillets. Top each serving with an equal amount of lemon slices, 1 sprig of thyme, $1/2$ tablespoon pine nuts, and 1 teaspoon white wine or vegetable broth. Follow the instructions for one of the parchment methods given (opposite). Repeat to form remaining parchment squares into pouches.

❏**bake pouches** Place pouches on a baking sheet. Bake for 15 minutes. (To test doneness, carefully cut into one of the pouches. Fillets should flake easily with a fork.) Let pouches rest on baking sheet for 5 minutes before serving.

❏**serve** Place each parchment pouch on a plate. Cut pouches open with kitchen shears. Remove sprigs of thyme and discard. Serve immediately.

we ❤ cooking!

how to use parchment

1 Beggar's Purse: Gather the edges of parchment around the filling to form a pouch. Wrap kitchen twine around the top and tie a knot (or a bow!), sealing the pouch.

2 Candy Wrapper: Place filling down in the center of a parchment square. Bring bottom and top edge of parchment together over filling and fold edges to seal shut. Twist the ends to seal and secure with twine. (Looks like a hard candy, right?!)

3 Traditional French Technique: Cut parchment into a heart shape. Place filling in center of one heart half and fold the other half over. Beginning at pointed end, fold the edge over all the way around the parchment to seal.

fish-on-a-stick

How often do you get to eat food on a stick? Probably not often enough! Our fish-on-a-stick is baked (which Lilly likes) and breaded (which I like), with a crispy pumpkin seed crust, because, well, why not? —Audrey

Hands-On Time: 20 min. Total Time: 27 min. Serves 4 (serving size: 3 skewers)

18 ounces cod or other lean white fish

12 (6-inch) skewers

1/4 teaspoon salt

1/4 teaspoon ground pepper

1/2 cup raw pumpkin seeds

1 lemon

1 tablespoon fresh chopped parsley

1 tablespoon olive oil

Low-fat tzatziki sauce (optional)

❑ **preheat oven** Preheat oven to 400°. Place a metal rack inside a rimmed baking sheet or baking pan. Set aside.

❑ **prepare fish** Cut fish into 12 equal-sized rectangles. Thread each piece onto a skewer. Sprinkle all over with salt and pepper.

❑ **make coating** Place pumpkin seeds in a food processor. Pulse until fine. Pour ground seeds into a shallow dish. Using a grater, grate the lemon zest. (You should have about 2 teaspoons.) Add lemon zest and parsley to ground seeds and stir until combined. Place olive oil in another shallow dish.

❑ **coat fish** Holding onto end of a skewer, dip fish into olive oil, then into seed mixture, turning to coat evenly. Lay prepared fish skewer on metal rack. Repeat with other pieces of fish.

❑ **bake fish-on-a-stick** Bake for 7 to 10 minutes or until pumpkin seeds are starting to brown and fish is firm.

❑ **serve with dipping sauce** Serve with tzatziki or other yogurt sauce on the side for dipping.

4'real?

It was the Native Americans who first used pumpkin seeds as an ingredient in food (and also medicine). Today, the crazy-healthy seed is still a go-to item in Mexican cooking—it's often ground up for sauces. So next time you carve a pumpkin, save those seeds!

make it look
delish!

If you make your dish *look* delicious, you'll help it *taste* delicious, too! Follow these tips.

go for classy! If you set the table, eating the meal becomes an *experience*. Start with a fresh tablecloth and nice napkins, and think about the time of year. Is it fall? Then add a bowl of mini pumpkins or gourds. Spring? A vase of just-picked flowers.

dress it up! Garnishes add more flavor to your food, and they can also be fancy, funny, and everything in between. Edible flowers look awesome on salads and soups, herb sprigs fancy-up bowls of pasta, and citrus zest makes desserts kind of sassy!

keep it small! Portion size is important not only for health reasons but also because too much food is kind of, well, unappealing. Match your portions to the person, or better yet, make individual portions, like our Mini Turkey Meatloaves (page 91).

get everyone on board! The feasts that are the most fun are the ones that get everyone at the table involved. We like to serve plain chicken curry with bowls of different toppings so guests can choose whatever they like (page 88). We also *love* chocolate fondue (page 173); we serve it with dippers like strawberries, bananas, marshmallows, and angel food cake bites. It's a huge hit every time!

we ♥ cooking!

pulled pork sliders

*Love pulled pork? These sliders are going to make you **dance**! Serve with slaw made with lacinato, a kale that's a little sweeter than usual.*

Hands-On Time: 50 min. Total Time: 5 hr. 50 min. Serves 8 (serving size: 2 sliders)

pork

2 jalapeño chiles

2 cups unsweetened pineapple juice

2 tablespoons lower-sodium soy sauce

1 tablespoon Worcestershire sauce

1 teaspoon salt

3 tablespoons packed brown sugar

2 tablespoons onion powder

1 tablespoon garlic powder

2 teaspoons dry mustard

2 teaspoons paprika

1 teaspoon chili powder

3 pounds pork shoulder, trimmed of excess fat

sliders

2 tablespoons mayonnaise

2 tablespoons apple cider vinegar

1/4 teaspoon salt

1/4 teaspoon black pepper

1 bunch lacinato kale (about 15 ounces)

16 whole wheat dinner rolls

❑ **mix cooking liquid** Cut jalapeños lengthwise into halves. Remove and discard stems and seeds. Finely chop jalapeños and place in a 5- to 6-quart electric slow cooker. Add pineapple juice, soy sauce, and Worcestershire sauce. Stir to combine. Set aside.

❑ **season pork** Mix salt, brown sugar, onion powder, garlic powder, dry mustard, paprika, and chili powder in a large non-reactive bowl. Place pork in bowl of spice rub and turn to coat all sides. Using your hands, press spice rub onto pork.

❑ **cook pork** Place pork in pot with pineapple juice mixture. Sprinkle any remaining spice rub into juice alongside pork. Cover and cook for 8 hours on LOW or 5 hours on HIGH.

❑ **reduce sauce** When pork is finished cooking, lift it from pot and place in a large bowl. Cover loosely with aluminum foil and set aside. Ladle liquid from slow cooker into a saucepan. Bring to a boil over high heat. Boil for about 20 minutes or until reduced by half.

❑ **make slaw** While sauce is reducing, combine mayonnaise, apple cider vinegar, salt, and pepper in a bowl. Set aside. Remove kale leaves from head. Cut away any tough stems and ribs and discard. Stack leaves and cut crosswise into thin slices to make chiffonade. Add kale to bowl with mayonnaise mixture and toss to coat. Set aside.

❑ **serve sliders** Using 2 forks, shred and pull pork apart. Pour 1 cup of the sauce over pulled pork and toss to coat. Reserve any remaining sauce to add as desired. Serve on wheat rolls with remaining sauce and kale coleslaw on the sliders or on the side.

wok-a-licious beef stir-fry

Too many cooks in the kitchen? Not possible with this recipe! There's plenty to do here, so start putting everyone to work!

Hands-On Time: 35 min. Total Time: 35 min. Serves 6 (serving size: ⅙ of mixture)

2 limes

6 tablespoons lower-sodium soy sauce

1 pound boneless sirloin steak, thinly sliced

2 teaspoons Chinese five-spice powder

1 teaspoon ground black pepper

1 cup sugar snap peas

2 carrots

1 yellow bell pepper

1 small red bell pepper

4 scallions, green tops included

1 stalk lemongrass, tough ends and outer leaves removed

2 garlic cloves

1 (1-inch) piece fresh ginger

1 (6-ounce) package rice noodles or bean thread noodles

2 tablespoons canola oil

☐**marinate meat** Juice limes into a small bowl or glass (you should have about 3 tablespoons). Mix in soy sauce. Set aside. Place sliced top sirloin in a large bowl or lock-top plastic bag and sprinkle evenly with Chinese five-spice powder and black pepper. Pour 6 tablespoons soy-lime mixture over the meat, toss, and set aside. Reserve remaining 3 tablespoons soy-lime mixture for noodles.

☐**prepare vegetables** Rinse all vegetables. Prepare vegetables, keeping them separate; cut snap peas and carrots into thin slices. Cut yellow and red bell pepper into julienne strips. (See technique, page 15.) Chop scallions, finely chop lemongrass, and mince garlic. Peel and grate the ginger. Set all aside until ready to cook.

☐**cook noodles** Prepare noodles according to package directions. Drain and return to pan used for cooking. With kitchen shears, cut the noodles several times to make them easier to eat. Pour remaining soy-lime mixture over noodles and toss to coat. Cover and set aside.

☐**cook meat and vegetables** Heat a large wok or sauté pan over high heat. Pour 1 tablespoon of the canola oil around the edges of the pan and heat until hot but not smoking. Using long-handled tongs or a wooden spatula, add beef and cook, tossing and stirring, for 4 minutes or until cooked through. Place meat and juices in a bowl and set aside. Add remaining 1 tablespoon oil to wok or sauté pan and heat for 30 seconds. Add the snap peas and carrots and cook, tossing and stirring, for 3 minutes or until slightly softened. Add the bell peppers and scallions and cook, tossing and stirring, for additional 3 minutes. (If the pan starts to get dry, add 2 tablespoons of water.) Add the lemongrass, garlic, and ginger. Cook, tossing and stirring, for an additional 2 minutes or until vegetables are tender.

☐**combine noodles and meat** Divide noodles among individual serving bowls. Return meat and its juices to the wok and stir for about 1 minute to thicken juices and reheat meat. Divide beef stir-fry mixture equally among noodles and serve.

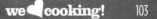

dad's quarter-pound blue cheese burgers

*Our dad makes blue cheese burgers that are **bonkers**, they're so good. We took his classic recipe and ran with it, adding our own twist. Thanks, Dad!*

Hands-On Time: 45 min. Total Time: 45 min. Serves 4 (serving size: 1 burger)

quick pickled red onion

1 lime

1/3 cup seasoned rice wine vinegar

1 tablespoon brown sugar

1 garlic clove

1 small red onion

burgers

1 ounce blue cheese, softened

1 ounce reduced-fat cream cheese, softened

1 tomato

1 cup fresh arugula

1 pound ground sirloin

1/2 teaspoon salt

1/2 teaspoon ground black pepper

4 (1 1/2-ounce) whole wheat burger buns or multigrain sandwich thins

☐ **make pickled red onion** Juice lime into a medium bowl. (You should have about 2 tablespoons.) Stir in vinegar and brown sugar. Using a meat pounder, pestle, or the flat side of a knife, crush the garlic clove and add to lime juice mixture. Cut onion in half through root end. Place cut side down on cutting board. Starting at tip, cut crosswise into thin slices. (You should have about 1 cup.) Toss onion with lime juice mixture. Cover and set aside.

☐ **prepare burger toppings** Place the blue cheese and cream cheese in a bowl. Mash together with a fork, dividing into 4 equal dollops. Set aside. Cut tomato into 4 equal slices. Rinse arugula and pat dry with paper towels or spin dry in a salad spinner. Set aside.

☐ **form and cook burgers** Using your hands, divide ground sirloin into 4 equal portions, forming patties about 1/2 inch wider than your buns. Press your thumb into the middle of each patty to make a 1-inch indent. Lightly sprinkle burgers all over with salt and pepper. Preheat a gas grill or grill pan to high heat. Place burger patties, indented side down, on grill rack or pan and grill for 3 to 4 minutes or until bottoms are browned. Turn patties over. Spoon 1 tablespoon cheese mixture into each indentation. Close grill or cover pan loosely with aluminum foil and cook an additional 3 to 4 minutes for medium or until done to your liking. Place burgers on a plate and cover with foil to keep warm.

☐ **toast buns** Place sandwich thins or buns, cut side down, on grill rack or pan. Grill for about 1 minute or until toasted.

☐ **assemble burgers** Drain the pickled onion in a small colander or strainer. To assemble burgers, place 1 patty on each bottom bun. Top each patty with desired amount of pickled onion, arugula, and tomato slices. Cover with top buns and serve.

lamb loin chops with lavender salt

*Have you ever cooked with lavender? It adds a little **somethin'-somethin'**.... Serve our lamb chops over polenta or brown rice, and add fresh lavender blossoms on top. Want more floral flavor? Mix two teaspoons of dried lavender with the salt instead of one.*

Hands-On Time: 17 min. Total Time: 30 min. Serves 4 (serving size: 2 chops)

1 teaspoon sea salt

1 large lavender sprig or 1½ teaspoons dried lavender

8 (3-ounce) lamb rib chops, trimmed

¼ teaspoon freshly ground black pepper

Olive oil cooking spray

❑**season chops** Preheat oven to 400°. Using a mortar and pestle or the back of a large spoon, crush sea salt and lavender together. Place lamb chops on a plate. Sprinkle lavender salt onto both sides of meat, rubbing it in with your fingers. Sprinkle chops all over with pepper.

❑**grill chops** Heat an oven-proof grill pan over high heat. Coat pan with cooking spray. When pan is hot, add chops. Sear 2 to 3 minutes on each side or until browned. Place the pan in the oven for 8 to 10 minutes or until chops are medium-rare.

❑**serve chops** Remove chops from the oven. Cover loosely with foil and let rest for 5 minutes before serving.

outrageous tries!

Flower power rocks! We love cooking with edible flowers. Not only do they look pretty, they also taste great. Nasturtiums are one of our faves, and we also like the blossoms from herbs like rosemary, chive, sage, basil, and thyme. You can use them in salads, pastas, chilled soups, or pretty much anywhere you want!

pizza supreme

Pizza is great for takeout, but when you make it at home, you have a blank canvas to play with. Go bold and "paint" your pizza with bright bell peppers!

Hands-On Time: 30 min. Total Time: 45 min. Serves 6 (serving size: 2 wedges)

1 (16-ounce) refrigerated fresh pizza crust dough

Cooking spray

2 teaspoons olive oil

1 (4-ounce) turkey Italian sausage link

1 cup sliced mushrooms

1 cup thinly sliced red bell pepper

1 cup thinly sliced orange bell pepper

1 cup thinly sliced onion

$1/4$ teaspoon crushed red pepper

3 garlic cloves, thinly sliced

$3/4$ cup lower-sodium marinara sauce

4 ounces fresh mozzarella cheese, thinly sliced

❑**prepare oven** Preheat oven to 500°.

❑**prepare dough** Roll dough into a 14-inch circle on a lightly floured surface. Place dough on a 14-inch pizza pan or baking sheet coated with cooking spray.

❑**cook sausage and veggies** Heat oil in a large nonstick skillet over medium-high heat. Remove casing from sausage. Add sausage to pan; cook 2 minutes, stirring to crumble. Add mushrooms, bell peppers, onion, crushed red pepper, and garlic; sauté 4 minutes, stirring occasionally.

❑**add toppings and bake** Spread marinara sauce over dough, leaving a 1-inch border. Arrange cheese evenly over sauce. Arrange turkey mixture evenly over cheese. Bake for 15 minutes or until crust and cheese are browned. Cut into 12 wedges.

white bean and quinoa chili

*Is it possible to make chili without a tomato base? Funny you should ask us that! We combined white beans with quinoa and simmered the whole thing in garlic, cumin, chili powder, oregano, and salt (did someone say **spicy**?!). FYI, our Parmesan-Veggie Drop Biscuits are drop-dead **divine** with this (page 114).*

Hands-On Time: 25 min. Total Time: 25 min. Serves 8 (serving size: 1/8 of mixture)

4 (15-ounce) cans cannellini beans

1 onion

3 carrots

1 tomato

1 pasilla or Anaheim chile pepper

1 tablespoon olive oil

3 garlic cloves

1 tablespoon chili powder

2 teaspoons dried oregano

2 teaspoons ground cumin

1 teaspoon salt

2 1/2 cups organic vegetable broth

2 tablespoons tomato paste

1/2 cup uncooked quinoa

1 avocado

Hot chile sauce, to taste (optional)

Fresh cilantro leaves (optional)

❑**prepare vegetables** Place beans in a colander, rinse well with cold water, and let drain. Set aside. Cut vegetables and set aside separately; chop onion. (You should have about 1½ cups.) Peel carrots and cut into ¼-inch slices. (You should have about 1 cup.) Cut tomato in ¼-inch dice. Cut pepper in half lengthwise and discard stem, seeds, and ribs. Chop finely.

❑**cook chili** Place a heavy-bottomed Dutch oven over medium-high heat. Add olive oil, swirling to coat bottom with oil. Add chopped chile and cook for 2 minutes or until fragrant, stirring occasionally. Add onion, carrots, and tomato. Cook for 5 minutes or until vegetables are beginning to soften, stirring often. While vegetables are cooking, peel and mince garlic. When vegetables have cooked for 5 minutes, add minced garlic, chili powder, oregano, cumin, and salt. Cook for 1 minute, stirring often. Add vegetable broth, tomato paste, and drained beans and stir until blended. Bring bean mixture to a boil over high heat. (While beans are coming to a boil, place quinoa in colander used for beans, rinse with cold water, and let drain.) Add quinoa to bean mixture and reduce heat to medium-low. Stir gently to mix, then simmer for about 10 minutes or until carrots and quinoa are tender.

❑**serve chili** Just before serving, peel, halve, and core avocado. Cut into ½-inch dice. Spoon chili into 8 shallow bowls, dividing it evenly. Top each serving with a sprinkling of avocado, hot sauce, and cilantro leaves, if desired.

 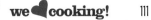

pick 'n' mix sides

Are you the kind of person who likes a whole bunch of different foods to choose from at mealtime? We get it— making a meal out of sides is a blast! And just in case you feel like going all out and cooking a feast, we have some suggestions about which sides go with which dishes. Bottom line? Sides rule!

parmesan-veggie drop biscuits

These drop biscuits are super simple, and spectacular. There's no kneading and no rolling—just mixing, blending, scooping, and dropping. They are totally dreamy with our White Bean and Quinoa Chili (page 111) and our Mini Turkey Meatloaves (page 91), and also in our lunch bags!

Hands-On Time: 25 min. Total Time: 60 min. Serves 12 (serving size: 1 biscuit)

1 carrot

½ zucchini

2 cups unbleached flour

2 teaspoons baking powder

¾ teaspoon kosher salt

½ teaspoon baking soda

½ cup shaved fresh Parmesan cheese

3 tablespoons minced fresh chives

¼ cup unsalted butter

¾ cup low-fat buttermilk (1%), chilled

❏ **cut vegetables** Mince carrot and zucchini. Set aside.

❏ **mix dry ingredients** Preheat oven to 375°. Line a baking sheet with parchment paper. Mix flour, baking powder, salt, and baking soda in a bowl. Add Parmesan cheese, chives, and minced carrot and zucchini. Toss to mix. Set aside.

❏ **blend wet and dry ingredients** Place butter in a small microwave-safe cup. Microwave at HIGH for 15 seconds or until melted. Pour buttermilk into a bowl. Stir in melted butter. Stir flour mixture into buttermilk mixture just until blended. Do not over-mix; mixture will be lumpy and loosely holding together.

❏ **bake biscuits** Drop dough by ⅓ cupfuls onto prepared baking sheet. Bake for 25 minutes or until golden brown. Remove from oven and let biscuits cool for 10 minutes on baking sheet, then serve.

how to make biscuits

1 Be sure to mince (finely chop) the carrot and zucchini. Don't be tempted to chop them in big pieces. Then combine flour and other dry ingredients in a bowl.

2 Stir flour mixture into buttermilk mixture just until blended. The mixture should be lumpy and loosely holding together. (It'll look better cooked, we promise!)

3 Use a large spoon or a ¹/₃-cup measuring cup to scoop batter. Drop dough onto baking sheet. Be sure to leave plenty of room between the biscuits because they *grow!* Give these beauties 10 minutes to cool and then taste your handiwork!

brussels sprouts our way

*Once upon a time, someone might have given you Brussels sprouts, and you might have **not** liked them. If that happened, we're sorry! But don't let that keep you from trying ours. We caramelize Brussels sprouts, which means we cook them until they're brown around the edges and super duper sweet. It's vegetable candy—seriously!*

Hands-On Time: 16 min. Total Time: 16 min. Serves 6 (serving size: ½ cup)

1 pound Brussels sprouts

1 bunch green onions

2 tablespoons butter

1 tablespoon olive oil

2 tablespoons brown sugar (optional)

½ teaspoon salt

⅛ teaspoon black pepper

❑ **prepare ingredients** Rinse Brussels sprouts, trim stem ends, and remove any wilted outer leaves. Cut Brussels sprouts into chiffonade. (See technique, page 15.) Set aside. Trim roots and dark green tops from green onions. Chop white and light green parts. (You should have about 1¼ cups chopped onions.) Set aside.

❑ **cook onions and sprouts** Heat butter and olive oil in a 12-inch skillet over medium-high heat. When butter melts, add green onions and cook, stirring, for 2 minutes. Add sprouts to pan and cook for 5 minutes until slightly brown around the edges, stirring often. Add brown sugar, if using, and cook for 1 minute or until sugar begins to caramelize. (Do not overcook; sprouts should remain bright green in color.)

❑ **season and serve** Remove pan from heat. Season with salt and pepper and serve.

Mom's EYE View

When the girls were young, they saw Brussels sprouts being shredded into strips—this is called chiffonade. They loved the way it looked and couldn't wait to try it, so we went to the farmer's market, bought some sprouts, and got out a chef's knife. With *very close* supervision in order to keep their fingers safe, they made endless variations of shredded sprouts for about a month ... until a new veggie caught their attention!

roasted sesame broccolini

*All righty, let's set the record straight! Broccolini is **not** broccoli. (This confused us at first, too, so don't feel bad.) They are in the same vegetable family, but Broccolini cooks faster than broccoli—it has a smaller "head" on a thinner stem. We like to roast Broccolini in the oven, because the heat makes it crisp and tender, not mushy (who likes mushy when it comes to eating vegetables?!). FYI, roasting is a great way to go with most veggies.*

Hands-On Time: 8 min. Total Time: 28 min. Serves 6 (serving size: $\frac{1}{6}$ of Broccolini)

1 pound Broccolini or broccoli rabe

2 teaspoons dark sesame oil

1 teaspoon canola oil

2 teaspoons white sesame seeds

2 teaspoons black sesame seeds

$\frac{1}{4}$ teaspoon kosher salt

☐ **prepare broccolini** Preheat oven to 350°. Line a rimmed baking sheet with parchment paper. Trim tough ends from Broccolini. Set aside.

☐ **coat with oil** Combine sesame oil and canola oil in a large bowl. Mix well. Add broccolini. Toss to coat with oil mixture. Sprinkle white and black sesame seeds over top. Toss to mix. Place broccolini on prepared baking sheet and sprinkle with salt.

☐ **roast** Bake for 20 to 25 minutes or until stems are tender. Serve immediately.

zucchini ribbon pasta

It's a pasta party on your plate—with no pasta! Your friends will chow down on this delish vegetarian dish so fast, they won't even realize that the "pasta" is ribbons of zucchini. If you want to get even wilder and crazier (woo-hoooo!), add any vegetable that you would eat with pasta.

Hands-On Time: 10 min. Total Time: 31 min. Serves 6 (serving size: 1 cup)

6 zucchini

3 shallots

1$^1/_2$ cups heirloom cherry tomatoes

$^1/_4$ cup water

1 tablespoon olive oil

$^1/_2$ teaspoon salt

$^1/_4$ cup fresh flat-leaf parsley, rinsed and stems removed

$^1/_4$ cup fresh grated Parmesan cheese

❑ **prepare vegetables** Wash, dry, and cut the ends off of the zucchini. Peel the zucchini with a wide vegetable peeler, if desired. Next, using the vegetable peeler, make zucchini ribbons; set aside. Slice the shallots and halve the tomatoes.

❑ **cook and serve vegetables** Heat a 9-inch sauté pan to medium-high, add $^1/_4$ cup water, and let it come to a simmer. Add the shallots and simmer, stirring occasionally, for about 7 minutes, until shallots are tender and water is absorbed. With the wooden spoon, move the shallots to the side of the pan, add olive oil, and stir. Add tomatoes and simmer, stirring occasionally, for another 5 minutes. Add the zucchini ribbons to the pan and cook for 4 to 5 minutes until softened, tossing occasionally with tongs. Add salt and parsley; toss again. Remove zucchini pasta to a serving platter. Sprinkle with cheese. Serve immediately.

rustic smashed potatoes

*Wish you could dive into this book and eat our smashed potatoes **right now**?! (So do we!) Here's the bottom line: Steam the potatoes—don't boil them. That way, they keep their flavor and soak up the broth. FYI, these spuds are **perfect** with our Lamb Loin Chops with Lavender Salt (page 107).*

Hands-On Time: 7 min. Total Time: 37 min. Serves 9 (serving size: ½ cup)

2 pounds Yukon Gold potatoes

¾ cup fat-free, lower-sodium chicken broth

3 ounces goat cheese, crumbled

2 tablespoons butter

1 tablespoon minced fresh chives

¾ teaspoon kosher salt

☐ **steam-cook potatoes** Cover the bottom of a large pot with 1 inch of water. Place potatoes in a steamer basket and lower into pot. Cover and bring to a boil over high heat. Reduce heat to medium-low and simmer for 30 minutes or until potatoes are tender.

☐ **smash potatoes** Transfer potatoes to a bowl. Using a potato masher or the back of a wooden spoon, smash potatoes. Continue smashing until no large chunks remain.

☐ **add seasonings** Add broth, goat cheese, and butter to potatoes. Smash again until evenly moist and a bit creamy. Sprinkle with chives and salt. Stir to mix, then serve.

outrageous tries!

Toppings with smashed potatoes are soooo good, they should be outlawed. Try ricotta cheese and sun-dried tomatoes, roasted sweet peppers and herbs, or (wait for it ...) cheddar cheese and salsa! (No joke!)

we ♥ gardening!

Here are some secrets—and confessions!—about one of our favorite spots in the world: the garden.

garden guests ...
We have a confession to make: We have gophers in our garden! And we now know exactly what they like to eat—potatoes and onions. They made a giant mess of our garden one summer, so we had gopher-proof raised beds put in. Now our veggies are safe (from gophers, at least!) for the whole growing season.

in pursuit of pomegranates
Our Grandpa Larry has a farm in northern California with two beautiful, gnarled old pomegranate trees. Whenever we visit him, we make a beeline for those trees and pick as many poms as we can get our hands on. We open up the best ones and eat the sweet jewel-like seeds until we literally can't eat anymore. Then, we take the rest inside and make icy-cold pomegranate lemonade!

lemony pick-it!
In the winter, our Pa (our dad's dad) picks the lemons off his Meyer lemon tree (even though it's covered with thorns!) and gives them to us. Lucky us, huh? He also takes some to his favorite bakery in town.

mini gardens
Even if you don't have a backyard (or any yard at all), you can still have a garden! All you need to grow herbs, lettuces, beans, and even some tomatoes is a sunny windowsill and determination. You'll love cooking with fruits and veggies that you grew yourself—it's a pretty cool feeling.

chopped salad with buttermilk-dill dressing

Do you like to have a little bit of everything on your fork at once? That's the point of a chopped salad! The bite-sized ingredients make it easy to get everything in one bite. A to-go tip: Pack your dressing separately and add it right before you eat.

Hands-On Time: 12 min. Total Time: 12 min. Serves 6 (serving size: 1⅓ cups)

dressing
½ small avocado

2 green onions

¼ cup fat-free Greek yogurt

½ cup low-fat buttermilk (1%)

1 tablespoon chopped fresh dill

2 teaspoons Dijon mustard

2 teaspoons sherry vinegar

½ teaspoon salt

¼ teaspoon freshly ground black pepper

salad
1 head romaine lettuce

1 yellow bell pepper

1 cucumber

2 carrots

½ pint cherry tomatoes

¾ cup canned chickpeas (garbanzo beans), rinsed and drained

⅓ cup toasted sunflower seeds or toasted pumpkin seeds

☐ **make dressing** Remove and discard avocado peel. Cut avocado in half and place in a blender or food processor. Trim and coarsely chop green onions, then add to avocado along with yogurt, buttermilk, dill, mustard, vinegar, salt, and pepper. Blend until smooth. Pour dressing into a container with a lid. Cover and refrigerate until ready to serve.

☐ **prepare salad** Separate lettuce leaves from head. Stack leaves, cut crosswise into slices, then chop. Place in a large serving bowl. Cut bell pepper in half through stem. Remove stem, seeds, and ribs. Chop pepper and add to bowl. Peel cucumber and carrots, then chop and add to bowl. Cut tomatoes into quarters and add to bowl. Add chickpeas and seeds to bowl. Toss gently to mix all ingredients.

☐ **serve salad** Add dressing to chopped vegetables and toss to coat. Serve immediately.

baby kale caesar salad

Ever wonder why the Roman emperor Julius Caesar has a seriously popular salad named after him? Well, we hate to break it to you, but ... he doesn't. The Caesar salad is named after an Italian chef based in California, Caesar Cardini. He invented "the Caesar" way back in 1924, making it with romaine lettuce. We like ours with super duper healthy baby kale.

Hands-On Time: 15 min. Total Time: 22 min. Serves 6 (serving size: 1²/₃ cups)

croutons
3 (1-ounce) slices sourdough bread

Cooking spray or 1 tablespoon olive oil

¼ teaspoon garlic powder

¼ teaspoon freshly ground black pepper

⅛ teaspoon smoked paprika

caesar dressing
2 garlic cloves, minced

⅛ teaspoon fish sauce

1 tablespoon light mayonnaise

1 tablespoon fresh lemon juice

1 teaspoon Worcestershire sauce

½ teaspoon Dijon mustard

½ teaspoon freshly ground black pepper

⅓ cup olive oil

salad
3 (1-pound) heads baby kale

½ cup shaved or grated Parmesan cheese

☐ **make croutons** Preheat oven to 450°. Cut bread slices into 1-inch squares. Spread squares in a single layer on a baking sheet. Spray lightly with cooking spray or drizzle with olive oil. Toss to coat with oil. Sprinkle bread with garlic powder, black pepper, and smoked paprika. Toss to coat with spices. Bake for about 7 minutes or until croutons are golden. Set aside.

☐ **make dressing** Place garlic and fish sauce in a non-aluminum salad bowl and mash together with a fork. Whisk in mayonnaise, lemon juice, Worcestershire sauce, Dijon mustard, and black pepper. Gradually whisk in olive oil. Set aside.

☐ **prepare kale** Separate leaves from heads of kale. Coarsely chop leaves. Rinse kale and spin dry in a salad spinner or pat dry with paper towels. Place in a salad bowl.

☐ **serve** Drizzle dressing over kale. Toss gently to coat evenly. Sprinkle croutons and Parmesan over top of salad. Toss gently to mix. Serve immediately.

outrageous tries!

Don't fear the kale! It's got more going for it than regular lettuce, like tons of iron, fiber, vitamins, and antioxidants, and also more flavor and crunch. The best choice for a salad is baby kale because the leaves are soft, mild, and bite-sized.

wikiwiki salad with mango dressing

Looking for a quick salad fix? Look no further. Wikiwiki (pronounced "wee-kee-wee-kee") literally means "hurry" in Hawaiian! You can make this simple salad in 10 minutes flat, and serve with grilled chicken or fish, if you like.

Hands-On Time: 10 min. Total Time: 10 min. Serves 6 (serving size: 1½ cups)

mango dressing
- ½ cup ripe fresh mango (1 small), rough chopped
- ¼ cup sweet onion, rough chopped
- ¼ cup rice vinegar
- 3 tablespoons olive oil
- 2 tablespoons honey

salad
- 6 cups spring greens, washed and dried
- 2 cups strawberries, rinsed and quartered
- ⅓ cup red onion, sliced
- 1 avocado, pitted and thinly sliced

☐ **blend dressing** Place mango, sweet onion, rice vinegar, olive oil, and honey in a blender. Blend until smooth, about 1 minute. Process on high speed for 60 seconds or until smooth.

☐ **toss salad** Place spring greens, strawberries, and red onion in a large salad bowl. Drizzle dressing over the salad and toss.

☐ **serve salad** Divide the salad into bowls, top each salad evenly with avocado, and serve.

Health Nut

This salad is so healthy, it's shocking! Just goes to show you that it doesn't take a ton of time to make something nutritious. Avocadoes are full of good fats, and mangoes and strawberries have antioxidants, fiber, and vitamin C. You'll shout "mahalo!" (thank you!) with each bite.

roasted cauliflower mash

*We can't believe it's not potato! This funky twist on mashed potatoes is **waaaay** lighter than the old standby but just as satisfying. Just ask our dad, who isn't cauliflower's biggest fan—he swears by our mash!*

Hands-On Time: 8 min. Total Time: 48 min. Serves 6 (serving size: $\frac{1}{2}$ cup)

1 head cauliflower (about $5\frac{1}{2}$ pounds)

2 tablespoons olive oil

$\frac{1}{2}$ teaspoon salt

3 slices center-cut bacon

3 green onions

3 ounces goat cheese, crumbled

❑**roast cauliflower** Preheat oven to 450°. Cut cauliflower into florets. Place florets on a rimmed baking sheet. Drizzle with olive oil and toss to coat. Sprinkle with salt. Bake for 40 minutes or until very tender.

❑**cook bacon** Meanwhile, place a skillet over medium-high heat. Lay bacon in skillet and cook, turning once, for 6 minutes or until crisp. Remove bacon from pan and let drain on paper towels. Crumble bacon.

❑**prepare toppings** Chop green onions, including green tops. (You should have about $\frac{1}{2}$ cup.) Crumble goat cheese. Set green onions and goat cheese aside.

❑**mash cauliflower** When cauliflower is done, place in a large bowl. Mash with potato masher to desired consistency.

❑**serve mash** Add green onion and goat cheese to mashed cauliflower and stir to combine. Sprinkle bacon over top. Serve immediately.

Health Nut

You'll be ahead of the game with our cauliflower mash because cauliflower has more vitamin C and vitamin K (yes, there *is* a vitamin K!) than potatoes. If you want to go *even healthier* than our recipe, use turkey bacon instead of regular bacon.

farro and winter vegetables

*This is our go-to dish for a cold winter night. It's the **ultimate** comfort food—warm and really hearty but with no frying, breading, or butter. (But don't get us wrong—there's definitely a time and a place for those things, too!)*

Hands-On Time: 8 min. Total Time: 48 min. Serves 5 (serving size: about 1 cup)

¹/₂ butternut squash

¹/₂ red onion

3 teaspoons olive oil, divided

¹/₂ teaspoon kosher salt, divided

1 cup uncooked farro

3 cups water

1 bunch green chard (about 6 ounces)

¹/₈ teaspoon black pepper

☐ **bake squash and onion** Preheat oven to 450°. Using a knife, remove peel from butternut squash. Discard seeds and cut pulp into ¹/₂-inch dice. Place in a 9 x 13–inch baking dish. Chop onion and add to squash in dish. Drizzle with 2 teaspoons olive oil and sprinkle with ¼ teaspoon salt. Stir to coat evenly. Bake for 20 minutes or until squash is tender.

☐ **cook farro** While squash mixture is baking, cook farro: Combine farro with 3 cups water in a saucepan over high heat. Bring to a boil. Reduce heat to medium-low and simmer 15 minutes or just until tender. Drain.

☐ **layer and bake casserole** Coarsely chop chard leaves. Rinse and spin dry in salad spinner or pat dry with paper towels. When squash is tender, carefully layer chopped chard over squash. Spread cooked farro evenly over chard. Return baking dish to oven and cook for 5 minutes or until chard is wilted.

☐ **serve casserole** Remove dish from oven and stir casserole gently until combined. Sprinkle with ¼ teaspoon salt and ¹/₈ teaspoon pepper. Drizzle remaining 1 teaspoon olive oil over top. Stir gently to mix, then serve.

Mom's EYE View

The girls have mastered many cutting techniques and know how to choose the right-sized tools in the kitchen. Having said that, I still feel more comfortable cutting winter squash for them. I halve it, then place it cut side down and remove the peel.

epic desserts

There is nothing ordinary about these desserts—they are definitely *epic*. As far as we can tell, the world pretty much divides into three kinds of dessert lovers—people who live for chocolate, people who would rather have fruity treats, and people who are happy to have anything, as long as it's dessert. No matter what category you're in, you're going to think this chapter is *sweeeeet!*

chocolate fudge pops

You have to be on your game to handle these fudge pops. It's not that they're hard to make—they're super easy, actually. The problem is that you have to figure out how to hide them in the freezer. Otherwise, they mysteriously disappear before you can eat one! —Audrey

Hands-On Time: 15 min. Total Time: 8 hr. 15 min. Serves 4 (serving size: 1 pop)

1 cup fat-free Greek yogurt

2 tablespoons unsweetened cocoa powder

1 cup evaporated low-fat 2% milk

1 teaspoon vanilla extract

3 tablespoons honey

❑ **prepare fudge mixture** Place all ingredients into a blender and blend on high until smooth, about 1 minute.

❑ **pour fudge mixture into molds and freeze** Pour the chocolate mixture evenly into each of 4 molds; pop on the top or add the wooden sticks. Place in the freezer 8 hours or until frozen solid.

how to make pops

1 Place all of the ingredients in a blender. Turn the blender on and blend for 1 minute. *Whirrrrrr* ...

2 Secure the popsicle molds in the stand. Slowly pour the fudge mixture evenly into each mold. Eat any drops that don't make it into the mold.

3 Place the mold tops on each mold and freeze for at least 8 hours. (No, you can't skip this step. Sorry! But it'll be worth it, we promise.)

4 To release the ice pops, simply dip the molds in steaming hot water for 5 to 10 seconds. The outer layer of the pops will soften, and they'll *pop* right out!

we ♥ cooking!   139

baked stone fruit with vanilla frozen yogurt

What do cherries, peaches, and apricots all have in common? Hard pits, aka, "stones," which is why they're called "stone fruits." Stone fruit is great on frozen yogurt, but stone fruit baked with brown sugar and spices on frozen yogurt is even better!

Hands-On Time: 10 min. Total Time: 1 hr. 45 min. Serves 4 (serving size: ½ cup frozen yogurt, about 1 cup fruit mixture)

1 cup cherries

4 apricots

2 peaches

¼ cup packed brown sugar

¼ teaspoon Chinese five-spice powder

2 cups vanilla low-fat frozen yogurt

☐ **prepare fruit** Preheat oven to 350°. Using a cherry or olive pitter, pit cherries, then cut cherries in half. Halve apricots, discard pits, and cut into quarters. Halve peaches, discard pits, and cut into eighths.

☐ **bake fruit** Mix brown sugar and Chinese five-spice powder in a small bowl. Place fruit in an 8-inch square baking dish. Add brown sugar mixture and toss to mix well. Bake for 35 minutes or until tender. Remove from oven and let cool.

☐ **serve fruit and yogurt** Spoon ½ cup yogurt into each of 4 small serving dishes. Top each serving with about 1 cup fruit mixture. Drizzle with any remaining fruit juices from bottom of baking dish and serve.

4'real?

Stone fruits are everywhere in the Mediterranean, but they weren't always. Traders brought them on an ancient trading route called the Silk Road. The fruits' Roman names may give us clues about where they came from originally: peaches (*persica*) from Persia, apricots (*armeniaca*) from Armenia, and cherries (*cerasus*) from Kerasun on the Black Sea.

blueberry galette

*This galette is **da bomb**—it only has eight ingredients and it's a breeze to make, but it looks super swanky. A galette is a flat, rounded pastry, and you can actually make it with whatever fresh fruit you have lying around. Make it for a party or a sleepover—it works for either one!*

Hands-On Time: 8 min. Total Time: 43 min. Serves 6 (serving size: 1 wedge)

½ (14.1-ounce) package refrigerated pie dough

1 teaspoon all-purpose flour

2 cups fresh blueberries, may substitute raspberries or blackberries

1 tablespoon coconut oil, melted

⅓ cup almond flour

¼ cup packed brown sugar

1 egg white

1 teaspoon turbinado sugar

❑**prepare pie dough** Preheat oven to 450°. Cut a piece of parchment about same size as baking sheet. Place parchment on a clean work surface. Unroll dough onto parchment paper and sprinkle with flour. Roll out dough into a round about ⅛ inch thick. Pick up edges of parchment paper to transfer parchment and dough to baking sheet.

❑**top pie dough** Place blueberries in a bowl. Add coconut oil and stir to mix. Set aside. Mix almond flour and brown sugar in another bowl. Pour flour mixture into center of rolled dough. Spread flour mixture evenly over dough, leaving a 1-inch border uncovered. Spread blueberries over flour mixture in a single layer. Fold edges of dough toward center, pressing gently to seal. Dough will only partially cover blueberries. Using a pastry brush, brush dough with egg white, then sprinkle with sugar.

❑**bake galette** Bake for 15 minutes or until edges are browned and juice is bubbly. Remove from the oven and let cool for 20 minutes. Cut into 6 wedges and serve.

Health Nut

Rumor has it that coconut helps your stomach digest, and blueberries keep your memory in tip-top shape. (Wait, what were we just talking about?)

chocolate cupcakes

We couldn't love chocolate more if someone paid us, so we think these chocolate-chocolate cupcakes are super swoony. The best part? Frosting them with a pastry bag that you can make yourself at home. You'll feel like a big-time cake boss.

Hands-On Time: 30 min. Total Time: 1 hr. 30 min. Serves 24 (serving size: 1 cupcake)

chocolate cupcakes

¹/₂ cup unsalted butter

2 large eggs

2 cups sugar

1¹/₂ cups nonfat evaporated milk

1 teaspoon vanilla extract

2 cups all-purpose flour

¹/₂ cup unsweetened cocoa powder

¹/₂ teaspoon baking soda

milk chocolate cream frosting

1 cup milk chocolate chips

¹/₄ cup unsalted butter

¹/₄ cup nonfat half and half

2¹/₂ cups sifted powdered sugar

☐ **preheat oven and make batter** Preheat the oven to 350°. Prepare muffin tins with cupcake papers and set aside. Using a mixer, beat the butter on high for 30 seconds and add eggs; stir until combined. With the mixer running on low, add the sugar, evaporated milk, and vanilla; scrape bowl and blend until smooth, about 2 minutes. Using a sifter into a bowl, sift the flour, cocoa powder, and baking soda together, stirring again to combine. With mixer on low, add the flour mixture to the wet ingredients. When flour is incorporated, turn the mixer to medium and mix for 2 minutes.

☐ **pour batter into pan and bake** Fill the cupcake papers half full and bake for 18 to 22 minutes or until a toothpick inserted in the center comes out clean. Cool on a wire rack.

☐ **make frosting and frost cakes** Melt the chocolate chips and butter in a saucepan over very low heat; whisk to combine. When melted, remove from heat and let stand for 2 minutes. Whisk in half and half and incorporate completely. Add powdered sugar and whisk until smooth. For a smooth frosted cupcake, frost while the frosting is still slightly warm or cool to room temperature and place in a freezer bag, cut the tip off, and pipe frosting onto cupcakes. (If too thick, add an additional tablespoon of half and half and whisk to combine.)

dream big!

The more we do with food, the more we want to do. Dream big, right? Check out our gustatory goals below. (Gustatory means "having to do with eating." Remember that word! It's totally going to show up on a test you take someday.)

Lilly

Learn to make Himalayan food

Learn to cook with one new ingredient each week.

Cook a 4-course meal over a campfire. (Too bad roasting marshmallows doesn't count as a course!)

Cook my favorite dishes for a huge crowd

Toss pizza dough with perfection. (Not quite there yet ... but someday!)

audrey

Cook and eat only vegetarian food for 3 weeks.

Once a week, taste a food I have never tried before.

Learn to carve vegetables into animal and flower shapes.

Cook Thanksgiving dinner by myself. (Is it even possible to keep other people out of the kitchen on Thanksgiving? I wonder ...)

Make dinner for the president of the United States ... and then have her on our show!

grandma's blondies

*When the holidays come, Lilly and I head to the kitchen to crank out batches and batches of Grandma's Blondies. (Thanks, Grandma!) We've tweaked her recipe by using pecans instead of walnuts. FYI, the best way to eat these is when they are still **warm** and the chocolate is **goooooooey** ... –Audrey*

Hands-On Time: 15 min. Total Time: 50 min. Serves 18 (serving size: 1 bar)

²/₃ cup butter

Cooking spray

2 cups all-purpose flour

1 teaspoon baking powder

¹/₂ teaspoon salt

¹/₄ teaspoon baking soda

1¹/₂ cups packed light brown sugar

2 large eggs

1 tablespoon vanilla extract

1 cup semisweet chocolate chips

³/₄ cups chopped pecans (optional)

☐ **melt butter** Place butter in a small saucepan or small microwave-safe bowl. Heat over low heat for about 1 minute or microwave at HIGH for about 20 seconds or until melted. Pour butter into large bowl of an electric mixer. Let cool.

☐ **mix dry ingredients** Preheat oven to 350°. Lightly coat a 9-inch square baking dish with cooking spray. Sift together flour, baking powder, salt, and baking soda into a bowl.

☐ **mix wet ingredients** Add brown sugar, eggs, and vanilla to butter in bowl. Beat for 1 minute on medium speed or until smooth.

☐ **combine wet and dry ingredients** Using a wooden spoon, stir flour mixture into butter mixture just until blended. Stir in chocolate chips and nuts, if using.

☐ **bake blondies** Pour batter into prepared baking dish and smooth top with a spatula. Bake for 25 minutes or until browned on top and crispy at edges but still slightly gooey in center. Let pan cool on a rack. When cool, cut into squares.

Dad's EYE View

One of the best parts of parenting kids who love to cook is sharing old family recipes with them. Teaching the girls how to make my mother's blondies—the same way she taught me—was a pretty special moment. Hopefully they'll pass along the recipe to their own children some-day, and they'll feel the same way.

meringue kisses

Yeah, you have to separate egg whites and get the seeds out of a vanilla bean for this recipe, but don't freak! You can do it. The vanilla bean is our secret weapon—the flavor will blow you away. Just choose one that is dark brown and bends but doesn't break—that's how you know it's good to go.

Hands-On Time: 9 min. Total Time: 2 hr. 9 min. Serves 60 (serving size: 1 cookie)

1 vanilla bean, split lengthwise (optional)

5 egg whites

1 cup sugar

¼ teaspoon salt

½ teaspoon vanilla extract

❑**preheat oven and prepare baking sheets** Preheat oven to 200°. Line two baking sheets with parchment paper.

❑**make batter** If using, gently split the vanilla bean with a knife and scrape out the seeds; set aside. In the bowl of a stand mixer or using a hand mixer, beat the egg whites on high speed until soft peaks form, about 1 to 1½ minutes. Turn the mixer down to low and slowly add the sugar. Next, add the salt, vanilla extract, and vanilla seeds. Turn the mixer back to high speed and beat until stiff peaks form.

❑**pipe batter onto baking sheets and bake** Spoon the batter into a large freezer bag or pastry bag and cut a ½-inch corner off of bag. Pipe 60 meringue kisses onto the parchment-lined baking sheets. Bake for 2 hours, remove from the oven, and let cool. Carefully remove the meringues from the parchment paper and store in an airtight container.

how to pipe meringue kisses

1 Place the bottom side of a large freezer bag in a bowl. Fold the top edges of the bag down around the outside of the bowl. Gently spoon the batter into the bag.

2 Once you've filled the bag, gently press the mixture towards the bottom of the bag. Using scissors, cut off a small corner of the bag. Easy, right?

3 Squeeze 60 kisses onto parchment paper. (It sounds like a lot, but it's really not—you'll see.) Bake for 2 hours and let cool on parchment paper before eating them—um, we mean, before storing them.

chocolate-coconut macaroons

*Chocolate + coconut = **miraculous macarooooooons**! These chunks of major deliciousness have just 7 ingredients, which makes them pretty easy to wrangle. After cooling them, pack them in an airtight container, and they'll last for a whole week. You'll love knowing that they're **waiting** for you ...*

Hands-On Time: 15 min. Total Time: 37 min. Serves 40 (serving size: 1 macaroon)

¹/₂ cup granulated sugar

³/₄ cup confectioners' sugar

2 tablespoons cake flour

3 tablespoons unsweetened cocoa powder

4 egg whites

1 teaspoon vanilla extract

2 cups shredded coconut

☐ **preheat oven and prepare baking sheets** Preheat the oven to 325° and line 2 baking sheets with parchment paper; set aside. Sift together into a bowl sugar, confectioners' sugar, cake flour, and unsweetened cocoa powder; stir with a fork to mix, and set aside.

☐ **make batter** Using a stand mixer, beat the egg whites on high for 60 seconds, until soft peaks form. Next, turn the mixer to low, add the vanilla, and slowly add in the dry ingredients one spoon at a time. Stop the mixer and gently scrape the sides with a spatula and resume adding the dry mixture until gone. Gently fold in the coconut 1 cup at a time, just until blended and egg whites stay fluffy.

☐ **drop batter onto baking sheets and bake** Drop a heaping tablespoon each onto the parchment paper about 1 inch apart. Bake for 22 minutes, let cool completely, and gently remove from the parchment.

party time

Par-ty! Par-ty! Par-ty! Parties are the best, right? We love to *go* to parties, we love to *crash* parties, but most of all, we love to *throw* parties. We've kind of got it down to a science at this point. Check out our planning strategies and our themed recipes, and then start writing that guest list!

how to throw a party!

What's the secret to hosting a killer bash? There are seven, actually: Pick a cool theme, choose sassy but simple decorations, serve awesome food, and plan great things for your guests to do. If you follow these simple steps, your next get-together will be a total blast, we promise!

1. Pick the theme! First question: What's the weather going to be like when you're having your party? Warm? Go for a picnic, block party, or a luau (leis and straw skirts for everyone!). Cold? Have a sleepover, a movie night, or a straight-up dance party where everyone comes dressed as their favorite singer!

2. Make the invites! Design invites that introduce your guests to the theme. Use your favorite art materials, channel your craft diva, and go all out.

3. Choose the location! What's the best place for your themed party? Your backyard is probably perfect for a luau. But if you need a roller rink or a bowling alley, then research a great location and have your guests meet there. Just keep your headcount in mind—"destination" parties can get pricey.

4. Plan the menu! Is it going to be tricky to pick food that your pals like **and** matches your theme? Then have your party between mealtimes, when you can serve different small bites and give your guests lots of options. Otherwise, have a mealtime party and serve some snacks first, followed by a main dish with a side, and then dessert.

we ♥ cooking!

5. Select the decs! And by decs, we mean decorations! Brainstorm your theme—what comes to mind? A red-checkered pattern for a picnic, popcorn bags for a movie night. Then choose a few colors that match your theme and *keep it simple.* Find things around the house that might work—Mom lets us pick flowers from the backyard and use plates and glasses from the kitchen cabinet.

6. Make the party favors! You'll want to thank your pals for coming by giving them a party favor to take home. Make sweet treats and pack them in mason jars or some other kind of cool, reusable container.

7. Plan the activities! What's a game or craft that matches your theme and that all your guests would have fun with? If you're having a picnic party, set up a decorate-your-own-cupcake table ... with sprinkles that look like ants!

When the big day arrives, remember that your guests take their cues from you, so have fun. If you're rockin' out at your own party, your guests totally will, too!

royal tea party

serves 6 to 8

raspberry sweet tea

maple-ginger soda

**citrus salad with balsamic honey
and pistachios**

fig and goat cheese canapés

cucumber tea sandwiches

lemon tea cookies

raspberry sweet tea

Hands-On Time: 10 min. Total Time: 20 min. Serves 12 (serving size: ½ cup)

6½ cups water

8 raspberry herbal tea bags

½ cup sugar (to reduce sweetness, use ⅓ cup sugar)

Crushed ice

¼ cup 1% low-fat milk

Raspberries for garnish

steep tea Bring 6½ cups water to a boil in a large saucepan, turn off the heat, and steep the tea bags for 8 minutes. Carefully remove the tea bags with tongs, placing them into a bowl, and discard.

sweeten and cool tea Add sugar to the tea and stir, bring to a boil, and turn off heat. Let tea cool in saucepan on the stove top.

serve tea To serve, fill glasses with crushed ice and pour ½ cup tea over the ice. Drizzle 1 teaspoon milk over the top of each glass of tea. Garnish with raspberries and serve.

maple-ginger soda

Hands-On Time: 7 min. Total Time: 47 min. Serves 8 (serving size: ½ cup)

2- to 3-inch piece fresh ginger

1 cup water

½ cup maple syrup

1 tablespoon vanilla extract

1 quart (32 ounces) sparkling water, chilled

make maple-ginger syrup Using a small knife, remove peel from ginger and discard. Cut ginger into thin slices. (You should have about ¼ cup sliced ginger.) Combine 1 cup water, maple syrup, and ginger slices in a medium pan. Bring to a boil over high heat. Reduce heat to medium-low and let simmer for 20 minutes. Remove from heat and let cool. Using a slotted spoon, remove ginger and discard. Stir in vanilla. Pour maple-ginger syrup into an airtight container and refrigerate until ready to serve.

mix soda Pour chilled sparkling water into a pitcher. Slowly pour in maple-ginger syrup and stir gently to mix. Pour over ice and serve immediately.

citrus salad with balsamic honey and pistachios

Hands-On Time: 17 min. Total Time: 17 min. Serves 8 (serving size: about 4 orange slices)

1/4 cup olive oil

1 1/2 tablespoons white balsamic vinegar

1 tablespoon honey

1/4 teaspoon kosher salt

1/3 cup pistachio nuts

6 navel or blood oranges

8 ounces jicama

make vinaigrette In a jar with a tight-fitting lid, combine olive oil, vinegar, honey, and salt. Cover and shake to mix well. Set aside.

prepare ingredients Preheat oven to 325°. Spread nuts in a shallow pan. Bake for 8 to 10 minutes until lightly toasted, stirring occasionally. Set aside. Peel oranges, removing any white pith. Cut oranges crosswise into 1/4-inch-thick round slices. Peel jicama, then grate.

arrange salad Arrange orange slices in a single layer on a large platter. Sprinkle grated jicama over orange slices. Sprinkle pistachios on top. Drizzle with vinaigrette and serve immediately.

fig and goat cheese canapés

Hands-On Time: 15 min. Total Time: 15 min. Serves 15 (serving size: 1 canapé)

5 slices oat nut bread

1/4 cup (about 2 ounces) goat cheese, softened

3 tablespoons fig jam

2 teaspoons lemon zest

1 teaspoon sliced fresh mint leaves

cut out bread rounds Place bread slices in single layer on a cutting surface. Using a 2-inch round cookie cutter, cut out 3 rounds from each bread slice, making 15 rounds total. (Use remaining bread for other uses. We use leftovers to make croutons.)

assemble canapés Neatly spread each round with 1 teaspoon goat cheese, then top with a heaping 1/2 teaspoon fig jam. Place canapés on a platter. Sprinkle evenly with lemon zest and mint. Serve immediately.

cucumber tea sandwiches

Hands-On Time: 17 min. Total Time: 17 min. Serves 16 (serving size: 1 sandwich)

1 English cucumber

1 stalk lemongrass

8 ounces $\frac{1}{3}$-less-fat cream cheese, softened

1 teaspoon grated lemon zest

$\frac{1}{3}$ teaspoon salt

8 (1-ounce) slices honey wheat bread

make cucumber filling Peel cucumber. Cut cucumber crosswise into slices ⅛ inch thick. Set aside. Trim away root end, tough tops, and outer leaves from lemongrass stalk. Mince lemongrass. (You should have about 1 tablespoon minced lemongrass.) Place cream cheese in a bowl. Add minced lemongrass, lemon zest, and salt. Stir to combine.

make sandwiches Spread cream cheese mixture over one side of each piece of bread. Arrange cucumber evenly over each of 4 cheese-topped bread slices. Top each with remaining 4 bread slices, cheese side down. Pressing firmly on top of each sandwich, cut away crust from all 4 sides. Cut each sandwich diagonally into quarters (criss-cross).

serve sandwiches Serve sandwiches immediately, or transfer to a platter, cover, and refrigerate for up to 3 hours.

we ❤ cooking!

lemon tea cookies

Hands-On Time: 14 min. Total Time: 26 min. Serves 30 (serving size: 1 cookie)

cookies
3/4 cup unsalted butter, at room temperature

1 cup granulated sugar

1 large egg

1 tablespoon grated lemon zest

1/4 cup lemon juice

2 1/2 cups all-purpose flour

1 teaspoon baking soda

glaze
1/2 cup powdered sugar, plus more for dusting

1 tablespoon lemon juice

mix wet ingredients Preheat oven to 375°. Place butter in a large bowl. Beat with a mixer at high speed for 30 seconds or until fluffy. Add sugar, egg, lemon zest, and lemon juice. Beat until combined, scraping down sides of bowl, if necessary.

mix dry ingredients Sift together flour and baking soda in a bowl.

combine wet and dry ingredients Add flour mixture to butter mixture and beat on low speed for 2 minutes or just until combined. Do not overmix.

shape dough Using palms of your hands, roll dough into 1-inch balls, placing them 2 inches apart on ungreased baking sheets.

bake cookies Bake for 10 minutes or until edges are golden brown.

mix glaze While cookies are baking, mix powdered sugar and lemon juice in a small bowl until smooth. Set aside.

glaze cookies When cookies are done, let cool for 2 minutes on pans. Remove from pans and place on wire racks. While cookies are still warm, brush glaze over tops using a pastry brush, then dust with powdered sugar. Let cookies cool completely, then serve.

we ♥ cooking!

valentines party
serves 4

savory grape and goat cheese
heart toasts

roasted beet and spinach salad

portabella-mushroom-
sweet potato pot pie

strawberry-basil heart tarts

savory grape and goat cheese heart toasts

Hands-On Time: 15 min. Total Time: 25 min. Serves 4 (serving size: 1 heart toast)

1 teaspoon grapeseed oil

$\frac{1}{2}$ teaspoon fresh rosemary, minced

$\frac{3}{4}$ cup seedless red grapes, cut in half

$\frac{1}{4}$ teaspoon salt

4 slices seeded whole grain bread

2 ounces goat cheese, softened

$\frac{1}{8}$ teaspoon black pepper, optional

cook grapes Heat a small sauté pan to medium-high heat, add the grapeseed oil and rosemary, and stir with a wooden spoon. Reduce the heat to medium and add the grapes and salt; sauté for 3 minutes while stirring occasionally.

toast bread and cut into heart shapes Toast the bread; remove the slices to a cutting board and using a 2- to $2\frac{1}{2}$-inch heart-shaped cutter, press into heart shapes. (We save the outer crusts to make croutons with.)

assemble toast Spread $\frac{1}{2}$ ounce of softened goat cheese on all 4 heart-shaped toasts. Divide and spoon sautéed grapes evenly onto the top of the goat cheese, drizzle a small amount of pan juices over the top of toast points, and sprinkle with the black pepper, if using. Serve immediately.

we ♥ cooking!

roasted beet and spinach salad

Hands-On Time: 14 min. Total Time: 54 min. Serves 6 (serving size: about 1 cup)

6 ounces white pearl onions

$1/2$ pound Chioggia beets

$1/2$ pound golden beets

3 garlic cloves

$2^1/2$ tablespoons olive oil, divided

4 cups fresh spinach

1 tablespoon white wine vinegar

$1/4$ teaspoon salt

$1/8$ teaspoon black pepper

2 ounces goat cheese

peel onions Bring a pot of water to a boil over high heat. Add onions and cook 1 minute. Drain in a colander placed in sink, then rinse with cold running water. Drain. Peel onions by pinching stem end of each onion, slipping them from skins. Discard onion peel. Set onions aside.

peel beets Trim off stem and root end of beets. Scrub beets under cold running water. Using a vegetable peeler, remove peel from beets and discard. Cut beets into 1-inch pieces.

roast vegetables Preheat oven to 400°. Place a piece of aluminum foil on a baking sheet. Cut garlic cloves into thin slices. Place garlic, beets, and pearl onions on foil. Drizzle 1 tablespoon of the olive oil over beet mixture and toss gently with your hands. Loosely fold sides of foil up to enclose vegetables and crimp to seal shut. Bake for 40 minutes or until beets are tender when pierced with a fork. Let cool, then refrigerate until ready to mix salad.

rinse and dry spinach Rinse spinach. Spin dry in a salad spinner or pat dry with paper towels. Place spinach in a salad bowl and set aside.

make vinaigrette In a small jar with a tight-fitting lid, combine remaining 1½ tablespoons olive oil, white wine vinegar, salt, and pepper. Replace lid and shake to mix well.

dress salad Drizzle vinaigrette over spinach and toss to coat. Add beet mixture and crumble goat cheese over top. Toss gently to mix. Serve in shallow bowls.

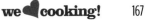

portabella-mushroom-sweet potato pot pie

Hands-On Time: 25 min. Total Time: 1 hr. 7 min. Serves 4 (serving size: 1 pot pie)

1 cup fresh or frozen peas

2 cups carrots, cut into $^1/_8$-inch-thick rounds

3 large portabella mushrooms, gills removed, cut into $^1/_2$-inch pieces

$^3/_4$ cup yellow onion, $^1/_2$-inch dice

2 tablespoons flour

1 tablespoon olive oil

$^3/_4$ teaspoon kosher salt, plus $^1/_4$ teaspoon

2 cups low-sodium vegetable stock

$^1/_4$ teaspoon ground cloves

1 bay leaf

2 tablespoons parsley, rough chopped

1 tablespoon fresh thyme, plus $^1/_2$ teaspoon

Olive oil cooking spray

1 medium sweet potato or yam, $^1/_8$-inch-thick slices

preheat oven and prepare filling Preheat oven to 350°. In a bowl, toss the peas, carrots, mushrooms, and onion with flour. Heat a large nonstick sauté pan to medium-high, and add olive oil. Add vegetable mixture and cook for 5 minutes, stirring occasionally. Sprinkle $^3/_4$ teaspoon salt over the vegetable mixture, and add the vegetable stock, ground cloves, bay leaf, parsley, and 1 tablespoon thyme. Bring to a low boil, and turn heat down and simmer for 15 minutes, stirring occasionally. Remove bay leaf.

fill ramekins and bake Place ramekins on a baking sheet and spray lightly with olive oil spray. Carefully spoon the vegetable mixture into the ramekins until ¾ full, including gravy. Place the slices of sweet potato on top of the vegetable mixture, overlapping them to cover. Spray with olive oil spray and sprinkle with ½ teaspoon thyme and ¼ teaspoon salt. Bake in the oven for 30 minutes. Then turn the oven to broil for 2 to 3 minutes until potatoes are browning on the edges. Remove from the oven and let cool for 10 minutes before serving each ramekin on a plate.

we ♥ cooking!

strawberry-basil heart tarts

Hands-On Time: 30 min. Total Time: 45 min. Serves 8 (serving size: 1 tart)

1¼ cups fresh strawberries

1 tablespoon fresh basil, minced

2 tablespoons brown sugar

1 teaspoon balsamic vinegar

3 tablespoons almond flour

2 sheets refrigerated pastry dough, thawed

1 egg

1 tablespoon turbinado sugar

preheat oven and prepare baking sheet Preheat oven to 350°. Line a baking sheet with parchment paper and set aside.

prepare strawberry filling Wash the strawberries and dice them; place in a medium-sized bowl. Add the minced basil, brown sugar, balsamic vinegar, and almond flour. Stir mixture together and set aside. Remove the pastry dough from the refrigerator and bring to room temperature. Crack the egg and separate the white from the yolk, discard the yolk, and lightly whisk the egg white; set aside.

prepare pie crust Lay the pastry dough out onto a lightly floured cutting board. Using a rolling pin, roll to ¼ inch thick. Using a 3½-inch heart-shaped or ring cutter, cut out 8 pieces of pastry dough and lay on the parchment. Repeat with other sheet of dough and leave on cutting board. Put 1 heaping tablespoon strawberry mixture on the center of 8 pastry cutouts. Lightly brush the edges with egg white and gently lay a pastry cutout evenly over the top. (Be sure not to press down.) Gently crimp outside edges of the heart with a fork, making sure to get all the edges. Repeat with the rest of the cutouts. Lightly brush the tops of the tarts with egg whites and sprinkle with sugar.

bake tarts Bake for 15 minutes or until golden brown. Remove tarts with a spatula to a wire rack to cool until warm to the touch and serve.

halloween
party
serves 6 to 8

vampire punch

pumpkin spice popcorn bags

salted chocolate fondue cauldron

fungi tartlets

ghoulish savory bread pudding

vampire punch

Hands-On Time: 5 min. Total Time: 5 min. Serves 28 (serving size: ½ cup)

1 large red beet

1 cup water

½ cup sugar

2 quarts unsweetened pineapple juice, chilled

1 quart sparkling water, chilled

1 (12-ounce) can frozen berry blend juice concentrate, thawed

make beet simple syrup Using a knife or vegetable peeler, peel beet. Cut beet into ½-inch-thick slices. Place beet slices in a saucepan. Add 1 cup water and sugar. Bring to a boil over high heat. Reduce heat to medium-low and simmer for 2 minutes or until syrup is bright red in color. Let cool. When syrup is cool, remove beet slices and discard.

mix punch Mix pineapple juice, sparkling water, juice concentrate, and beet simple syrup in a punch bowl. Serve over ice in small glasses.

pumpkin spice popcorn bags

Hands-On Time: 7 min. Total Time: 7 min. Serves 12 (serving size: 1 cup)

½ cup popcorn kernels, divided, or 12 cups popped popcorn

¼ cup unsalted butter

1½ teaspoons pumpkin pie spice

1 teaspoon sugar

¼ teaspoon salt

pop popcorn kernels If using popcorn kernels, pop them in 2 batches: place ¼ cup kernels in a brown paper lunch bag. Fold top over twice to seal in popcorn. Place bag on side in a microwave oven. Microwave on HIGH or on popcorn setting until there are about 3 seconds between pops, about 2 minutes. Pour popcorn into a large bowl and set aside. Repeat to pop remaining corn. If using popped popcorn, place it in a large bowl.

make spiced butter Place butter in a small microwave-safe bowl. Microwave on HIGH for 10 to 15 seconds or until melted. Stir in pumpkin pie spice, sugar, and salt.

mix popcorn and spices and serve Drizzle spiced butter mixture over popcorn while stirring constantly until coated. Fill individual goodie bags with about 1 cup popcorn per bag. Serve immediately.

salted chocolate fondue cauldron

Hands-On Time: 16 min. Total Time: 16 min. Serves 16 (serving size: ¼ cup fondue mixture)

6 pints strawberries

1 pint blueberries

8 bananas, cut into (1-inch) pieces

2 cups (1-inch) pineapple cubes

2 cups nonfat half and half

4 ounces 60% cacao bittersweet chocolate

4 cups semi-sweet chocolate chips

1 teaspoon almond extract

½ teaspoon sea salt

prepare fruit skewers Arrange strawberries, blueberries, bananas, and pineapple in separate serving bowls. Cover and refrigerate until ready to serve.

make fondue Combine half and half and bittersweet chocolate in a saucepan over low heat. Heat, stirring constantly with a whisk, for about 2 minutes or until chocolate is melted and mixture is smooth. Remove pan from heat. Add chocolate chips. Whisk gently for about 1 minute or until melted and smooth. Stir in almond extract.

serve fondue Pour chocolate mixture into a fondue pot set over low heat or ladle into individual serving bowls. Sprinkle top(s) with pinch of salt. Serve immediately alongside bowls of fresh fruit and skewers for dipping. Guests should thread their choice of fruit onto a skewer, then dip fruit into chocolate fondue.

fungi tartlets

Hands-On Time: 20 min. Total Time: 35 min. Serves 6 (serving size: 2 tartlets)

Olive oil spray

2 tablespoons water

1 cup shiitake mushrooms, thinly sliced (about 3 ounces)

1 tablespoon minced red onion

$^1/_2$ teaspoon salt, divided

1 sheet prepared pie dough, thawed

1 egg

$^1/_2$ cup fat-free evaporated milk

$^1/_8$ teaspoon black pepper

1 tablespoon minced fresh parsley

$^1/_3$ cup grated Gruyère cheese

preheat oven and prepare pan Preheat the oven to 400°. Spray mini tart pan or muffin tin with olive oil spray.

cook mushrooms In a small sauté pan, heat 2 tablespoons of water over medium-high heat. Add the mushrooms and cook for 2 minutes, stirring occasionally. Next add the onion to the pan and sprinkle with ¼ teaspoon salt. Cook for 1 additional minute. Remove from heat and set aside.

prepare dough On a lightly floured cutting board, roll out the pie dough to ⅛ inch thick. Using a 2½-inch round cutter or open end of a drinking glass, cut rounds of dough as close together as you can. Gently press the rounds into the mini tart pan or muffin tin. Set aside.

make filling and bake tarts In a bowl, whisk together the egg, evaporated milk, ¼ teaspoon salt, black pepper, and parsley. Pour egg mixture evenly divided into the tart or muffin tin. Evenly divide the cheese into each egg mixture, then divide the mushroom mixture evenly on top of the cheese. Be careful not to press down on the mushrooms. Bake for 10 to 11 minutes or until edges are golden brown and it is slightly moist-looking in the center. Let cool for 5 minutes in the pan, carefully remove to a platter, and serve.

we ♥ cooking!

ghoulish savory bread pudding

Hands-On Time: 15 min. Total Time: 1 hr. 10 min. Serves 6 (serving size: ½ cup)

3 green onions

2 garlic cloves

8 ounces mild Italian sausage, casings removed

Olive oil cooking spray

12 ounces whole wheat sliced sourdough bread

3 ounces pepper jack cheese

2 ounces cheddar cheese

1¼ cups 1% low-fat milk

1 (4-ounce) jar sliced sweet pimentos, drained

2 eggs

½ teaspoon kosher salt

¼ teaspoon black pepper

cook sausage Chop green onions, including green tops. (See technique, page 15.) Mince garlic. Set green onions and garlic aside. Heat a nonstick sauté pan over medium-high heat. Crumble sausage meat into pan. Cook for 5 minutes or until browned, stirring occasionally. Add green onions and garlic. Cook for 1 minute longer, stirring often. Remove from heat and set aside.

prepare pudding mixture Preheat oven to 350°. Coat a 2-quart baking dish with olive oil cooking spray. Tear or cut bread into 2-inch pieces. Set aside. Shred jack and cheddar cheeses. (You should have about ¾ cup shredded jack cheese and ½ cup shredded cheddar cheese.) Place shredded cheeses in a large bowl. Add milk, pimentos, eggs, salt, and pepper to cheese in bowl. Stir with a whisk until blended. Stir in sausage mixture. Add bread pieces and stir gently until evenly coated and most of the liquid is absorbed.

bake pudding Pour bread mixture into prepared baking dish. Bake for 45 minutes or until puffed and golden brown. Let cool for 10 minutes and serve.

italian block party
serves 6 to 8

pomegranate-honey italian soda

banner melon fruit skewers

pinzimonio crudité boats

sweet pepper and
prosciutto bruschetta

mandarin italian ice

pomegranate-honey italian soda

Hands-On Time: 5 min. Total Time: 40 min. Serves 6 (serving size: 1⅓ cups)

4 cups unsweetened
  pomegranate juice

½ cup honey

6 cups sparkling water

make syrup Combine pomegranate juice and honey in a saucepan. Bring to a boil over high heat. Reduce heat to medium-low and simmer for 35 minutes or until mixture is reduced by half, stirring occasionally. Remove from heat and allow to cool completely. Store in an airtight container in the refrigerator until ready to serve.

make sodas To make each soda, fill glasses with ice and pour ⅓ cup of pomegranate-honey syrup into each glass. Fill each glass with 1 cup sparkling water and serve.

banner melon fruit skewers

Hands-On Time: 21 min. Total Time: 1 hr. 21 min. Serves 24 (serving size: 1 skewer)

1 honeydew melon

1 cantaloupe

½ cup fresh mint leaves

½ cup honey

¼ cup lime juice

24 (6-inch) wooden
  skewers

cut melon Cut melons in half and remove seeds. Cut melon into long wedges about 1½ inches wide at bottom. Cut off and discard melon rind. Cut melon wedges crosswise into triangular pieces about 1½ inches thick.

add dressing Stack mint leaves. Cut crosswise into thin slices to make chiffonade. You should have about ¼ cup chiffonade. (See technique, page 15.) Place mint in a large lock-top plastic bag. Add honey and lime juice. Mix well. Add melon, close bag, and turn gently to coat melon with dressing. Refrigerate 1 to 2 hours.

prepare skewers Remove melon pieces from dressing and thread onto 6-inch skewers, alternating one type of melon then another. Place skewers on platter. Pour remaining honey mixture over skewers.

we ♥ cooking!

pinzimonio crudité boats

Hands-On Time: 11 min. Total Time: 11 min. Serves 6 (serving size: 1 boat)

dressing

2 tablespoons olive oil

1 teaspoon orange zest

2 tablespoons fresh
orange juice

$1/2$ teaspoon chopped
fresh thyme

$1/4$ teaspoon sea salt

$1/8$ teaspoon ground
black pepper

boats

1 head heart of romaine

1 cucumber

1 red or yellow
bell pepper

1 cup baby carrots

1 cup snow peas
or snap peas

1 cup small cauliflower
florets

make dressing Combine olive oil, orange zest, orange juice, thyme, salt, and pepper in a small jar with a tight-fitting lid. Shake until well mixed. Set aside.

prepare salad ingredients Trim ends of romaine head. Cut in half lengthwise and separate into leaves. Set aside. Cut cucumber in half lengthwise. Using a spoon, scrape out seeds and discard. Cut cucumber, bell pepper, and carrots into julienne strips. (See techniques, page 15.) Coarsely chop peas and cauliflower. Place prepared vegetables in a bowl. Drizzle dressing over vegetables. Toss to coat evenly.

assemble romaine boats Divide vegetable mixture evenly among lettuce leaves. Serve immediately.

sweet pepper and prosciutto bruschetta

Hands-On Time: 22 min. Total Time: 44 min. Serves 22 (serving size: 1 bruschetta)

1 small yellow bell pepper

1 small orange bell pepper

1 small red bell pepper

½ small red onion

2 tablespoons olive oil, divided

1 teaspoon salt

¼ teaspoon ground black pepper

1 tablespoon white balsamic vinegar

4 ounces thinly sliced prosciutto

1 sourdough baguette

1 teaspoon minced garlic

cut peppers and onion Cut peppers in half through stem. Remove stem, seeds, and ribs. Chop peppers and set aside. (You should have about 2¼ cups chopped peppers.) Chop onion and set aside. (You should have about ½ cup chopped onion.)

prepare pepper-onion topping Heat 1 tablespoon olive oil in a sauté pan over medium-high heat. Add peppers and cook for 2 minutes or until beginning to soften, stirring often. Add onion, salt, and black pepper and cook for 8 minutes or until onion is beginning to brown at edges, stirring occasionally. Remove from heat and stir in vinegar. Set aside.

make prosciutto crumble While vegetables are cooking, preheat oven to 400°. Line a baking sheet with parchment paper. Lay prosciutto slices in a single layer on prepared baking sheet. Bake for about 10 minutes or until fat turns golden and meat darkens slightly. Let prosciutto cool on baking sheet. When cool, crumble prosciutto into a bowl. Set aside.

make toasts Cut baguette on diagonal into slices ¼ inch thick. Place bread slices in a single layer on baking sheet. Bake for 12 minutes or until edges are golden brown. Let cool.

serve bruschetta Mix garlic and remaining tablespoon of olive oil in a small bowl or cup. Using a silicone brush or pastry brush, brush each slice of toasted bread with garlic olive oil. Top with a generous amount of sweet pepper mixture and a sprinkle of crispy prosciutto. Arrange bruschetta on a platter and serve immediately.

mandarin italian ice

Hands-On Time: 15 min. Total Time: 3 hr. 15 min. Serves 12 (serving size: $^3/_4$ cup)

1 cup sugar

1 cup water

3$^1/_2$ cups mandarin or tangerine juice

make simple syrup Combine sugar and water in a saucepan. Bring to a boil over high heat for 1 to 2 minutes or until sugar has dissolved, stirring occasionally. Remove from heat and let cool.

mix in juice Pour mandarin juice into a 9 x 13–inch glass casserole dish. Slowly add simple syrup and stir to combine.

freeze and scrape Carefully place dish in freezer. Freeze for 1½ hours. Remove dish from freezer and scrape mixture with a fork to fluff it, working from the center to edges. Return dish to freezer and freeze for an additional 1½ hours. Remove dish and scrape ice again.

serve Spoon ice into bowls or paper cones. Serve immediately.

acknowledgments

We needed some help on our cooking adventure, and we have many people to thank for their support and encouragement along the way! To our mom who said "yes" when we begged her over and over again to not have to wait until we were grown-ups to be chefs. To our dad, "Captain Safety," who taught us that baking is precise and grilling can be dangerous. You are the best dad. To Kathryn, the best sister, thank you for trying everything we make. To the rest of our family, who are our biggest fans. The gatherings and special holidays have inspired cooking and entertaining since we could walk and talk. A special thanks to Grandma Betty for listening for hours on the phone about our hopes and dreams. And Grandma Helen, for sharing her love for cooking and her special top secret recipe (not so secret anymore)!

Thank you to the friends and mentors who believed in us, like Chef Charles Holmes, who bought us our first knives and taught us the proper way to use them. Our big Italian family (almost) the Amorosos, especially Kristi for our first fresh pasta lesson. (Sorry about the mess.) And Steve Weissman, who met us in the front yard and hosted us at his restaurant, and helped build our first website. Our neighbors, Dan and Eileen Gillman, who are prepared at a moment's notice for a spontaneous photo shoot with all of their fun props. Our teachers and principal, Mr. Reno, who have helped and supported our learning in and out of school. All of our friends, especially Ella, Torence, and Marie, who help us keep it real! Our bestie, Chef Bob Blumer, who keeps our feet firmly planted on the ground. We can't thank Elizabeth Eckholt enough for sharing her knowledge on fresh ingredients and cooking.

(The days spent with you cooking are our best!) Emily Charrier, thank you for your friendship and your kind words. David Bowling, thank you for giving us our first cover. You made fish faces popular again. Darius and Sarah Anderson, for giving us the priceless gift of classes at your top-notch Ramekins Culinary School. Green String Farm, Sonoma Farmers Market, and Sonoma County Farm Bureau, you have made it easy for two kids to love fresh food. Meg Smith, our food adventure is captured forever from the very beginning because of your amazing photos and your belief in us. (THANK YOU, we heart you!)

Thank you to our fairy godmother Nancy Seltzer for noticing two ambitious girls who had a dream and have made it happen for them. We love you! Thank you Michael Ullman, Scott Schwimer, Meg Smith, and Adam Gurzenski for helping us keep our cooking dreams going. Lisa Atwood, who helped us put down our words for everyone to read! James Carriere and your team made our look through the oven a fun and perfect cover. A special thank you to Romney Steele and Leigh Nöe. (David and Chuck, you went all out for us on the roof!)

Lastly, people who have made our cookbook dream a reality, our book agency Janklow and Nesbit, especially Cullen Stanley, thank you. Our warm and most helpful editor, Andrea Kirkland, who guided us through the process. Erica Sanders-Foege, Leah McLaughlin, Felicity Keane, Christopher Rhoads, Frances Higginbotham, and photography staff from the Oxmoor House publishing team, our cookbook is a thousand percent everything we imagined, thank you! Everyone at Cooking Light! To our readers, thank you for letting us share our recipes with you and your family!

index

we ♥ cooking!

we ♥ cooking!

nutrition facts

	calories	total fat (sat fat) g.	protein g.	carb g.	fiber g.	iron mg.	sodium mg.	calc mg.
apricot cheese poppers p. 52	177	12.5 (2.2)	4.8	14	2.5	1	90	59
baby kale caesar salad p. 129	235	15.5 (3)	8	20	2	2.5	269	206
baked stone fruit with vanilla frozen yogurt p. 140	330	5.5 (2.5)	11	63	2.5	2.5	59	303
banana almond butter french toast sandwich p. 32	228	8.5 (1)	8.5	33	5.5	1.5	228	69
banner melon fruit skewers p. 178	53	0 (0)	0.5	14	1	0	15.5	8
berry berry warm quinoa cereal p. 25	297	10 (3)	11.5	42.5	5.5	2.5	50	176
blueberry galette p. 143	259	14 (6)	4	33	2	0.5	186	24
brussels sprouts our way p. 116	95	6.5 (3)	2	6.5	3	0	255	30
cannellini bean and corn salad pita pocket p. 70	196	5 (1)	9	32	4	2	460	60
caprese open-faced sandwich p. 69	188	10 (4.5)	10	17	2	1	248	13
chai spiced milk steamer p. 46	165	5 (3)	8	23	1	0	116	309
chicken and sausage paella p. 92	376	12.5 (3)	31	34	3.5	2	766	35
chicken curry bar p. 88	432	16 (7.5)	28	46	5	2.5	433	62
chilaquiles and eggs p. 29	261	17 (4)	10	20	4	1.5	346	67
chocolate-coconut macaroons p. 153	42	1 (1)	1	7.5	0.5	0	18	1
chocolate cupcakes p. 144	264	9 (5)	3.5	45	1	1	30	64
chocolate fudge pops p. 138	129	1 (0)	9	21	0	0	90	198
chopped salad with buttermilk-dill dressing p. 126	150	7 (1)	7	17	7	2	352	94
citrus salad with balsamic honey and pistachios p. 161	160	9 (1)	2	20	4	1	63	54
creamy dreamy tropical smoothie p. 22	135	2 (1.5)	4	28	1	0.5	47	124
cucumber tea sandwiches p. 162	73	3.5 (2)	2	8.5	1	0.5	179	18
dad's quarter-pound blue cheese burgers p. 104	341	11 (5)	28	37	4.5	3	917	109
devilish eggs p. 58	125	10 (2.5)	7	1	0	1	200	33
double-dip guacamole and tortilla chips p. 57	175	13 (1)	2	21	7.5	0.5	296	27
easy-peasy soup with lemon zest p. 85	150	3 (2)	7	21	6.5	2	525	21
farro and winter vegetables p. 134	212	4 (0.5)	7	41	6.5	3	269	80
fig and goat cheese canapés p. 161	50	1 (0.5)	2	8	0	0	72	37
figgy chewy granola wheels p. 50	202	10 (3.5)	4.7	24	6	1	154	60
fish-on-a-stick p. 97	265	15 (2)	28	4	1	2	220	27
fungi tartlets p. 174	70	3 (1.5)	5	5	0.5	0.5	270	0
ghoulish savory bread pudding p. 175	425	23 (10)	20	30	4	3	880	265
grandma's blondies p. 149	253	11 (6.5)	3	38	1	1	179	36
grown-up grilled cheese p. 66	264	15 (7)	13	23	3	1.5	265	330
jammin' oat muffins p. 41	183	6 (0,5)	3	30	1	1	106	80
kale leaf frittatas to go p. 26	146	8 (3.5)	12	6	1	2	395	176
lamb loin chops with lavender salt p. 107	220	10 (3.5)	30	0	0	2	665	20

we ♥ cooking!

	calories	total fat (sat fat) g.	protein g.	carb g.	fiber g.	iron mg.	sodium mg.	calc mg.
lemon tea cookies p. 163	117	5 (3)	1	17	0.5	0.5	45	4
mandarin italian ice p. 181	96	0 (0)	0	24	0	0	1	13
maple, bacon & egg crêpes p. 30	195	8 (3)	10	20.5	0	1	315	98
maple-ginger soda p. 160	104	0 (0)	0	27	0	0	14	79
meringue kisses p. 150	15	0 (0)	0	30	0	0	14	0
mini sesame asian tostadas p. 62	44	0.5 (0)	1.5	9	2	0.5	5	60
mini turkey meatloaves p. 91	351	15 (5)	37	18	1	3.5	927	102
munch mix p. 49	201	12 (5)	4.5	19	4	1	49	83
pad thai spring rolls p. 76	243	9 (1.5)	12	30	2	1.5	217	42
parmesan-veggie drop biscuits p. 114	138	5.5 (3.5)	4	18	1	1	314	86
pinzimonio crudité boats p. 179	50	3 (0)	0	5	5	0	110	50
pizza supreme p. 108	320	10 (4)	13	44	3	4.5	760	20
pomegranate-honey italian soda p. 178	178	0 (0)	1	45	0	0	21	28
portabella-mushroom-sweet potato pot pie p. 168	177	6 (0.5)	5	28	7	2	620	64
puffy popovers with raw apple compote p. 38	215	4.5 (2)	9	34	1.5	2	291	99
pulled pork sliders p. 100	348	17 (6)	30	16	1	2.5	580	58
pumpkin seed tapenade bruschetta p. 61	117	3.8 (0.5)	3.5	18	2.5	1	414	14
pumpkin spice popcorn bags p. 172	67	4 (2.5)	1	7	1	0	50	3
radiatore minestrone soup p. 82	259	6 (1)	9	43	6.5	3.5	740	99
ranch-style potato hash p. 42	172	5.5 (2)	6	25	3	1	388	84
raspberry sweet tea p. 160	35	0 (0)	0	9.5	0	0	2	5
red velvet pancakes p. 37	255	5.5 (3)	9	44	1.5	2	594	210
roasted beet and spinach salad p. 167	133	8 (2)	4	14	3	1.5	223	46
roasted cauliflower mash p. 133	228	14.5 (8)	11	7	3	1	488	77
roasted sesame broccolini p. 119	54	3.3 (0.5)	3	4	0	1	102	55
rotisserie chicken salad lettuce cups p. 78	185	8 (1)	18	4	1	0.5	350	46
rustic smashed potatoes p. 123	118	3.5 (2)	3	18	1	1	243	5
salted chocolate fondue cauldron p. 173	371	16.5 (9)	4	62	7.5	2.5	109	60
savory grape and goat cheese heart toasts p. 166	137	5.3 2.4	6	16.5	2	1	310	50
sole in parchment pouches p. 94	274	15 (2.5)	30	6	3	3	650	102
strawberry-basil heart tarts p. 169	64	2 (0.5)	2	10	1	0.5	33	17
sweet pepper and prosciutto bruschetta p. 180	44	2 (0.5)	2	5	0.5	0.5	285	1
thanksgiving wrap p. 81	307	13 (7.5)	15	33	2	3	570	146
twin chefs sushi rolls p. 72	411	15 (4)	24	45	5.5	1.5	653	52
vampire punch p. 172	82	0 (0)	1	20	0	0.5	12	20
white bean and quinoa chili p. 111	250	6.3 (1)	12	39	11	3.5	629	105
wikiwiki salad with mango dressing p. 130	172	12 (2)	1	18	5	1	24	16
wok-a-licious beef stir-fry p. 103	291	8 (2)	17	37	3	3.5	603	65
zucchini ribbon pasta p. 120	75	3 (0.5)	3	10	2	1	18	35

we ♥ cooking!

nutritional analysis

how to use it and why

Glance at the end of any *Cooking Light* recipe, and you'll see how committed we are to helping you make the best of today's light cooking. With chefs, registered dietitians, home economists, and a computer system that analyzes every ingredient we use, *Cooking Light* gives you authoritative dietary detail like no other magazine. We go to such lengths so you can see how our recipes fit into your healthful eating plan. If you're trying to lose weight, the calorie and fat figures will probably help most. But if you're keeping a close eye on the sodium, cholesterol, and saturated fat in your diet, we provide those numbers, too. And because many women don't get enough iron or calcium, we can help there, as well. Finally, there's a fiber analysis for those of us who don't get enough roughage. Here's a helpful guide to put our nutritional analysis numbers into perspective. Remember, one size doesn't fit all, so take your lifestyle, age, and circumstances into consideration when determining your nutrition needs. For example, pregnant or breast-feeding women need more protein, calories, and calcium. And women older than 50 need 1,200mg of calcium daily, 200mg more than the amount recommended for younger women.

in our nutritional analysis, we use these abbreviations

sat	saturated fat	CHOL	cholesterol
mono	monounsaturated fat	CALC	calcium
poly	polyunsaturated fat	g	gram
CARB	carbohydrates	mg	milligram

daily nutrition guide

	Women ages 25 to 50	Women over 50	Men ages 24 to 50	Men over 50
Calories	2,000	2,000 or less	2,700	2,500
Protein	50g	50g or less	63g	60g
Fat	65g or less	65g or less	88g or less	83g or less
Saturated Fat	20g or less	20g or less	27g or less	25g or less
Carbohydrates	304g	304g	410g	375g
Fiber	25g to 35g	25g to 35g	25g to 35g	25g to 35g
Cholesterol	300mg or less	300mg or less	300mg or less	300mg or less
Iron	18mg	8mg	8mg	8mg
Sodium	2,300mg or less	1,500mg or less	2,300mg or less	1,500mg or less
Calcium	1,000mg	1,200mg	1,000mg	1,000mg

The nutritional values used in our calculations either come from The Food Processor, Version 10.4 (ESHA Research), or are provided by food manufacturers.

we ♥ cooking!

metric equivalents

The information in the following charts is provided to help cooks outside the United States successfully use the recipes in this book. All equivalents are approximate.

cooking/oven temperatures

	Fahrenheit	Celsius	Gas Mark
Freeze Water	32° F	0° C	
Room Temp.	68° F	20° C	
Boil Water	212° F	100° C	
Bake	325° F	160° C	3
	350° F	180° C	4
	375° F	190° C	5
	400° F	200° C	6
	425° F	220° C	7
	450° F	230° C	8
Broil			Grill

liquid ingredients by volume

$^1/_4$ tsp	=					1 ml
$^1/_2$ tsp	=					2 ml
1 tsp	=					5 ml
3 tsp	=	1 Tbsp	=	$^1/_2$ fl oz	=	15 ml
2 Tbsp	=	$^1/_8$ cup	=	1 fl oz	=	30 ml
4 Tbsp	=	$^1/_4$ cup	=	2 fl oz	=	60 ml
5$^1/_3$ Tbsp	=	$^1/_3$ cup	=	3 fl oz	=	80 ml
8 Tbsp	=	$^1/_2$ cup	=	4 fl oz	=	120 ml
10$^2/_3$ Tbsp	=	$^2/_3$ cup	=	5 fl oz	=	160 ml
12 Tbsp	=	$^3/_4$ cup	=	6 fl oz	=	180 ml
16 Tbsp	=	1 cup	=	8 fl oz	=	240 ml
1 pt	=	2 cups	=	16 fl oz	=	480 ml
1 qt	=	4 cups	=	32 fl oz	=	960 ml
				33 fl oz	=	1000 ml = 1 l

dry ingredients by weight
(To convert ounces to grams, multiply the number of ounces by 30.)

1 oz	=	$^1/_{16}$ lb	=	30 g
4 oz	=	$^1/_4$ lb	=	120 g
8 oz	=	$^1/_2$ lb	=	240 g
12 oz	=	$^3/_4$ lb	=	360 g
16 oz	=	1 lb	=	480 g

length
(To convert inches to centimeters, multiply the number of inches by 2.5.)

1 in	=			2.5 cm	
6 in	=	$^1/_2$ ft	=	15 cm	
12 in	=	1 ft	=	30 cm	
36 in	=	3 ft	= 1 yd	=	90 cm	
40 in	=			100 cm	= 1m

equivalents for different types of ingredients

standard cup	fine powder (ex. flour)	grain (ex. rice)	granular (ex. sugar)	liquid solids (ex. butter)	liquid (ex. milk)
1	140 g	150 g	190 g	200 g	240 ml
$^3/_4$	105 g	113 g	143 g	150 g	180 ml
$^2/_3$	93 g	100 g	125 g	133 g	160 ml
$^1/_2$	70 g	75 g	95 g	100 g	120 ml
$^1/_3$	47 g	50 g	63 g	67 g	80 ml
$^1/_4$	35 g	38 g	48 g	50 g	60 ml
$^1/_8$	18 g	19 g	24 g	25 g	30 ml

ISBN-13: 978-0-8487-0424-7
ISBN-10: 0-8487-0424-X
Library of Congress Control Number: 2014943715

Printed in the United States of America
First Printing 2014

Oxmoor House

Editorial Director: Leah McLaughlin
Creative Director: Felicity Keane
Art Director: Christopher Rhoads
Executive Food Director: Grace Parisi
Senior Editors: Andrea C. Kirkland, M.S., R.D.;
  Erica Sanders-Foege
Managing Editor: Elizabeth Tyler Austin
Assistant Managing Editor: Jeanne de Lathouder

We Heart Cooking!

Project Editor: Emily Chappell Connolly
Editorial Assistant: April Smitherman
Junior Designer: Frances Higginbotham
Assistant Test Kitchen Manager: Alyson Moreland Haynes
Recipe Developers and Testers: Wendy Treadwell, R.D.;
  Tamara Goldis, R.D.; Stefanie Maloney; Callie Nash;
  Karen Rankin; Leah Van Deren
Food Stylists: Victoria E. Cox, Margaret Monroe Dickey,
  Catherine Crowell Steele
Photography Director: Jim Bathie
Senior Photographer: Hélène Dujardin
Senior Photo Stylists: Kay E. Clarke, Mindi Shapiro Levine
Senior Production Managers: Greg Amason, Sue
  Chodakiewicz

Contributors

Writers: Lisa Atwood, Louise Rozett
Assistant Project Editor: Megan Thompson
Copy Editors and Proofreaders: Marathon Production
  Services
Nutrition Analysis: Keri Matherne, R.D.
Indexer: Nanette Cardon
Fellows: Laura Arnold, Kylie Dazzo, Nicole Fisher,
  Elizabeth Laseter, Loren Lorenzo, Anna Ramia,
  Caroline Smith, Amanda Widis
Food Stylists: Elizabeth Eckholt, Erica Hopper, Ana Kelly,
  Romney Steele
Photographers: James Carriere, Meg Smith, Becky Stayner
Photography Assistant: David Escalante
Photo Stylists: Mary Clayton Carl, Leigh Nöe
Photo Stylist Assistant: Chuck Luter

Cooking Light®

Editor: Scott Mowbray
Creative Director: Dimity Jones
Executive Managing Editor: Phillip Rhodes
Executive Editor, Food: Ann Taylor Pittman
Executive Editor, Digital: Allison Long Lowery
Senior Food Editors: Timothy Q. Cebula, Cheryl Slocum
Senior Editor: Cindy Hatcher
Nutrition Editor: Sidney Fry, MS, RD
Associate Editor: Hannah Klinger
Assistant Editor: Kimberly Holland
Assistant Food Editor: Darcy Lenz
Art Directors: Rachel Cardina Lasserre, Sheri Wilson
Designer: Hagen Stegall Baker
Assistant Designer: Nicole Gerrity
Tablet Designer: Daniel Boone
Photo Editor: Amy Delaune
Senior Photographer: Randy Mayor
Chief Food Stylist: Kellie Gerber Kelley
Assistant Prop Stylists: Lindsey Lower, Claire Spollen
Food Styling Assistant: Blakeslee Wright Giles
Test Kitchen Manager: Tiffany Vickers Davis
Recipe Testers and Developers: Robin Bashinsky,
  Adam Hickman, Deb Wise
Production Director: Liz Rhoades
Production Editor: Hazel Reynolds Eddins
Production Coordinator: Christina Harrison
Copy Director: Susan Roberts McWilliams
Copy Editor: Kate Johnson
Office Manager: Alice Summerville
Intern: Gina Yu
CookingLight.com Editor: Mallory Daugherty Brasseale
CookingLight.com Assistant Editor/Producer: Michelle Klug

Time Home Entertainment Inc.

President and Publisher: Jim Childs
Vice President and Associate Publisher: Margot Schupf
Vice President, Finance: Vandana Patel
Executive Director, Marketing Services: Carol Pittard
Publishing Director: Megan Pearlman
Assistant General Counsel: Simone Procas

Photo Credits

Courtesy of: 54 bottom right, Suzi Q Varin; 55 top left, Frankie Franken. **Getty Images:** 12 top right, Tina Rupp; 12 bottom left, AID/a.collectionRF; 12 bottom right, Andrew Pini; 14 top, TS Photography; 16 top left, Hiroshi Higuchi; 16 middle left and 54 middle right, mstay; 16, 34-35, 54-55, 74, 98, 124, 156-157, textured backgrounds, Classix; 54 top right, Hong Li; 54 bottom left, Alexandra Rowley; 55 top left, Jonathan Kantor; 55 middle right, Floortje; 55 bottom left, Carlos Daniel Gawronski; 74 top right, Hideki Yoshihara/Aflo; 124 right, Rosemary Calvert; 171 top, Mary Rudakas; 171 middle, Jojo100; 177 top, Linda Steward; 177 middle, Anna Bryukhanova; 177 bottom, Getty Images. **iStock:** 124 bottom, FrankvandenBergh; 159 top, Andrew_Howe; 159 bottom, Bebebailey; 171 bottom, Nic_Taylor. **Shutterstock:** 35 bottom left, Ammit Jack; 55 middle left, Helga Esteb; 74 bottom right, Mahathir Mohd Yasin; 98 middle left, Kim Nguyen; 124 top left, Kerry L. Werry; 124 middle left, Suzanne Stevenson. **Thinkstock:** 16 bottom left, Natikka; 34 top right, Matt_benoit; 34 bottom right, Mastamak; 35 far top right, Hanzl; 74 left, Jon Wightman; 159 middle, Elena Belousova; 165 top, Nik_Merkulov; 165 middle, Marina Zakharova; 165 bottom, Thinkstock.